52
WAYS TO
MAKE THIS
YOUR BEST
YEAR YET

52 WAYS TO MAKE THIS YOUR BEST YEAR YET

Todd Temple

Thomas Nelson Publishers
Nashville

Published in Nashville, Tennessee, by Oliver-Nelson Books, a division of Thomas Nelson, Inc., Publishers, and distributed in Canada by Word Communications, Ltd., Richmond, British Columbia.

The Bible version used in this publication is the HOLY BIBLE, NEW INTERNATIONAL VERSION®. Copyright © 1973, 1978, 1984 by International Bible Society. Used by permission of Zondervan Publishing House. All rights reserved.

Printed in the United States of America.

ISBN 0-8407-9198-4

■ Contents

Wisdom

Social Action

Simple Living

■ Introduction

It takes twenty years to make an overnight success.
                                            —Eddie Cantor

For some people, this will be a spectacular year. They'll win the lottery or lose forty pounds or get discovered by Hollywood or discover the cure for a disease. A single act of fortune, brains, or guts will turn their lives from mediocre to magnificent.

This book is for the *rest* of us. Our success and happiness in life won't come from the big things but from the countless small victories we achieve along the way. That's what this book is all about: small victories. Here are fifty-two of them, arranged in no particular order.

So pick an idea—any idea—and get to work. When you've conquered the task, celebrate. You're a victor! While you're reveling in your success, pick another and charge at it. Each small victory reminds you of your ability to win another.

Go get 'em!

Relationships

1. Look Up a Long-Lost Friend

Yes'm, old friends is always best, 'less you can catch a new one that's fit to make an old one out of.
—Sarah Orne Jewett

Chances are, some of the most important moments of your past are stored in photo albums, home movie reels, or videocassettes. But the best memory storage isn't film or magnetic tape. It's an old friend.

Memory Maker His memory was recording your life *between* the Kodak moments, capturing change and growth better than any time-lapse camera. And he wasn't just an eyewitness; he was a part of the action—shaping and being shaped by your character, actions, and beliefs.

You were a camera for him, too. You remember things that he has long forgotten. You may recall kind gestures or noble acts that you never thanked him for. Maybe there were things you wish you had said, but you didn't have the language to express them. And of course, there was that time he walked through the school corridor with toilet paper stuck to the bottom of his shoe. He needs to hear that story again, don't you think?

Maybe it's time to look up one of these long-lost friends. Even if you share little in common now, you can still celebrate and learn from the moments that helped to make you. Make some calls; do some detective work; track him down. You'll both be the better for it.

Detective Tips   Here are a few friend-finding tips to get you started:

- Call the local directory assistance. If he isn't listed, get the numbers of others with the same last name.

- Call your high school. Your class's reunion committee can help.

- Call other old friends. It's a small world. Another friend has probably contacted one you've lost track of.

- Call professional organizations. If he set out to be a plumber, lawyer, accountant, actor, doctor, or pilot, his association or union has an address.

2. Heal an Old Wound

'Twas thine own genius gave the final blow,
And helped to plant the wound that laid thee low.

—Byron

Conventional wisdom holds that the pain of the past will fade as our memory of painful incidents fades. The memory is a ship sailing over the horizon, carrying the pain with it. It's a comforting and hopeful metaphor. Too bad it doesn't work that way.

A great wound in the past—a broken or abusive relationship with a parent, sibling, friend, or spouse; a violent act; or a money or career crisis—is more like a boomerang. Toss it off with denial and it comes right back to you. If you try really hard, you can fling it very far from your consciousness. But when it comes back—and it will, months or years or decades later—it flies into your life with overwhelming force.

Let's get back to the medical analogy. There's really only one way to prevent a deep wound of the past from crippling us. Open it up, clean it out, and then let it heal properly. How long that takes depends on the size of the wound, how long it has gone untreated, how hard you want to work, and so on. You won't heal yourself in a day, and you probably won't do it in a week. But you *can* get the healing process started. Here's how.

Start with the Symptoms You may not be aware of an old wound, or you may think that you've put it behind you. But something isn't quite right inside. At first you thought it was a mood or a phase, but the feeling won't go away. Maybe you feel sad, isolated, numb, angry, or hopeless. Figure out what doesn't feel right.

Assess the Damage Whatever the symptoms are, they affect your everyday life. What hinders your self-image, work, friendships, marriage, family relationships, attitude, and so on? How would things be different if the symptoms stopped? This line of questioning will help you discover the depth of the wound and motivate you to get healthy.

Find Out What Wounded You—and Why If you hurt but don't know why, it could be something you've worked very hard to block out. To discover it, you have to rummage through the attic of your mind, triggering memories that trigger more memories. If you think the hurt started in your childhood, siblings and old friends can really help. They remember things you don't, and they may have a clue to your problem but have waited for you to broach the subject. A trained counselor can help, too. Once you've found the source, you're halfway home.

Feel the Pain Anger and grief are important parts of the healing process. You may have been denied the opportunity to feel these emotions; now is your chance. More than anything, you need to talk to someone—a trusted friend or counselor—who can help you acknowledge the pain and comfort you as you finally feel it.

Your confidant can help you determine the wisdom of another step: expressing your feelings to the person who hurt you. If you do, don't expect much back. The person is probably hurting, too, but won't be anywhere near your point in the healing process. If a meeting is unwise or impossible, write a letter that goes unsent. List the things you appreciated about the person, the things that hurt, and how each has affected you.

Forgive For most people, forgiving is the hardest part. An unforgiving heart is self-destructing. The anger you hold for someone eventually infects the love you have for another. Sometimes the toughest person to forgive is yourself.

Live Smart A wound that has gone untreated leaves you vulnerable to similar injury, even after you treat the wound. Learn from the past and prevent a reinjury.

Work to Heal Others This is the victory celebration. Now that you've made the journey, use your empathy and wisdom to guide others through it.

3. Join the Generations

Everyone has been a child. All can understand through muffled memory how childhood was. But none has been old except those who are that now.
—Bert Kruger Smith

Grandparents do a lot more than spoil the grandkids and provide free baby-sitting. Members of the oldest generation provide members of the youngest with the sense that they belong to something *permanent:* a family that outlives death and divorce.

Unfortunately, as our lives become busier and family members move farther apart, we have fewer opportunities to gather the extended family and connect with our heritage.

Whether you're the grandparent, the child, or the grandchild, you can help carry on the sense of family in your clan by bringing the generations together. Here are some activities for family gatherings of three or more generations. Get one of them on the calendar. Make the calls this week to work it out.

Hand-Me-Down Cooking It's hard to believe that humans survived for thousands of years without benefit of cookbooks. Each generation handed down cooking knowledge to the next—the family traditions and cultural heritage went along for the ride. Make sure this process doesn't stop now. Have the elder play master chef; the young ones are his protégés. Prepare and serve an old family recipe.

Namesakes At a family gathering ask each generation to explain why they chose the names they did for their children—who was named for whom and so on. Ask grandchildren to think of what they'd like to name their own children and why.

Story Time Ask the oldest member to tell the youngest a story she remembers hearing from her parents or grandparents. If it's a good one, ask her to tell it again on another occasion. At the next gathering, switch hats; let one of the youngest re-tell the story while the others listen.

Three-Story Views Ask a question and let each generation answer it. For example, ask everyone to describe his elementary school. This gives Gramps another opportunity to lengthen the distance and increase the depth of snow he trudged through to get to school; you can talk about how girls were sent home for wearing pants; and your daughter can describe the computers she used in kindergarten. Other three-story topics include most embarrassing moment, what you wanted to be when you grew up, earliest memory, favorite song, best friend, first job, and best vacation.

Visit Her Childhood   If possible, take a family trip to where a grandparent grew up. Have her show grandchildren where she played, worked, and attended school. A walk down memory lane will be fun for her—and it will give grandchildren a sense of their heritage.

4 ■ Say You're Sorry

Human beings are perhaps never more frightening than when they are convinced beyond doubt that they are right.

—Laurens Van der Post

Most people know the language of apology. Just walk through a crowded gathering and you'll hear: "Excuse me," "I beg your pardon," "Forgive me," and "I'm sorry." We're quick to say these things when we've just stepped on someone's toe or forgotten his name or bumped her hand into the chip dip.

But when we've truly hurt someone—broken a promise, vandalized a trust, injured the body or soul—the words don't come so quickly.

Sometimes we hold on to our apology as a kind of reward that we'll release as soon as the other person admits to *his* fault in the matter. Of course, he, too, has posted a reward—for *our* admission. Welcome to the standoff.

If we injured the person intentionally to retaliate for something she did, we hold back our apology as a kind of parole to be granted when we decide she has been punished enough.

Or maybe we withhold our apology because we want to forget that we were wrong. We feel bad enough already; bringing up the topic is only going to make us feel worse.

Whatever our reasons for withholding an apology, something deep inside won't let us rest until we come clean. Here's how.

Hear the Other Side "Whatever I did to hurt you, I'm sorry." It sounds nice, but it doesn't do much for the injured party. If you can, ask the person to tell you what you did and how it hurt. Don't argue or deny or blame. Just listen.

Think . . . Feel . . . Regret Admit to yourself what you did wrong. Try to imagine how the person feels—the pain, the anger, the frustration.

Express Your Sorrow Now you're ready to express your regret. Acknowledge your actions and how they hurt the person. Say you're sorry.

Ask for Forgiveness Expressing your regret works to heal the injured person's heart. Asking for forgiveness works to heal your own.

Change Your Ways Up till now you've been cleaning up the past. Now work on being less messy in the future.

Do you owe someone an apology? Do both of you a favor and say you're sorry. Get started today.

5. Say When

"I'll never cry for you again," said I. Which was, I suppose, as false a declaration as ever was made, for I was inwardly crying for her then, and I know what I know of the pain she cost me afterwards.

—Pip

You're having dinner with a friend. When she dishes the food onto your plate, she tells you to "say when." It's a simple concept: one person telling another when enough is enough.

Wouldn't relationships be a lot simpler if everybody knew when to say when? Some of us seldom say it at all. We let others decide the quality and depth of our relationships. In a romantic relationship, we let a partner determine the level of physical intimacy. At work, we sign our lives over to the boss. In friendship, we suppress our needs and spend our time and money catering to the whims of our friends.

We pay for our lack of limits eventually. One day we wake up empty and in pain because we've given everything to another and now there's nothing left to give. That sets off a chain reaction: the person who bled us dry now senses our resentment— even though we held out an arm and pointed to where to stick the needle. Desperate for someone to help us recover from the pain, we jump into another relationship. We give it everything we have because we can't afford to lose it. Then we wake up empty again, and we're back where we started.

If this sounds familiar, it's time to set some limits:

- Decide how many hours you can work without harming your personal life.

- Evaluate your friendships and spend time with persons who know how to give and take.

- In a romantic relationship, figure out what you want and what you can give, and set some limits—physically, emotionally, and on how much time you can spend together.

Take time this week to set some limits. Figure out when to say when. Then when you reach your limit, say when.

6. Thank a Teacher

A teacher affects eternity; no one can tell where his influence stops.

—Henry Adams

Out of the dozens of teachers you had in school, you probably remember a few who were exceptional: the English teacher whose reading list opened new worlds to you each week; the history teacher whose classroom discussions were cut way too short by the bell; the physics teacher who had you measuring the size of the earth with a stepladder and a stopwatch—and loving it.

They taught you volumes of facts and figures, but most of all, they inspired you to ask questions, think big, and dream bigger.

Send a Letter It's time to thank one. Call your school and find out if she's still there. If not, tell the people in the office what you're up to and ask if they can help you find her. When you've tracked her down, write a letter.

What Do You Say? Tell her

- who you are.

- what year you attended her class.

- what you're up to now.

- why she was special.

- what you remember.

- how she has affected your life.

If she's still teaching, you'll inspire her to give present students what she gave you. If she has retired, your letter will be an unexpected and welcome retirement gift.

So what are you waiting for? Call your alma mater today.

7. Crack a Smile

Nothing like a little judicious levity.
—Robert Louis Stevenson

A real smile is a cause-and-effect phenomenon. When you feel good on the inside, your face lights up. But it's possible to reverse the process: wipe a smile onto your face and you *may* start to feel better on the inside.

It's Contagious   You've seen enough fake grins to know this isn't always true. Some people can smile even when they're mad enough to scream. But a smile can induce joy if you're ready for it. Experiment with this trick on the phone, where you can't see the other person's face. Work your face into a smile, then listen for your voice to change.

It works even better face-to-face. At the supermarket checkout, don't just say, "Thank you." Look the person in the eye and smile. Your face lights up his, which triggers your good feelings. Yawns aren't the only contagious behaviors.

Tricky Places to Eke Smiles Try to get others to smile in these places:

- Elevators
- Streets of a big city
- Your den while everyone is watching *Terms of Endearment*
- A bank during a robbery
- During a news report about the economy
- A Midnight Madness sale
- Life rafts surrounded by sharks
- A children's photo studio during prime napping hours

Count 'Em Up Make this "Smile Induction Week." Keep a daily tally of the number of people you can get to smile simply by smiling first. Award yourself double tallies for tricky-place smiles.

8. Knock Out the Negs

Whatever is true, whatever is noble, whatever is right, whatever is pure, whatever is lovely, whatever is admirable—if anything is excellent or praiseworthy—think about such things.

—Apostle Paul

Negative numbers are pretty powerful: if you multiply a positive number by a negative one, you always end up with a bigger negative. Negative words are just as powerful: add them to any comment and they affect the whole conversation.

Of course, negative words have their place. There's no point in pretending that everything is always wonderful. But we give them too much airtime, especially with their prolific breeding habits and pernicious ability to infect our attitude. Cut down on the negatives in your thoughts and conversations this week. Here's a trick to help you.

Pick out all the positive words from the Bible verse quoted above (it's Philippians 4:8), and write them on an index card or a small piece of paper: *true, noble, right, pure, lovely, admirable, excellent, praiseworthy.* Carry the card in your pocket or purse. As you pick up the phone or walk up to greet someone, review the list. Before you open your mouth, check to be sure the words in your brain are compatible with the words from the list.

9. Carry On the Traditions

History is a pact between the dead, the living, and the yet unborn.

—Edmund Burke

We hear a lot about the disintegration of the family. What we need is some glue. Family traditions bind families through the generations. They remain the same while everything around us is changing.

Learn the traditions of your family. Ask grandparents and other older relatives to recall the holiday traditions of their childhoods; pass them on to your children. Where there is no tradition, create one.

Instant Traditions

Sing fest   Sing before every family holiday meal. Search out songs that carry out the theme of the holiday ("Over the River and Through the Wood," "The Star-Spangled Banner," "The Old Rugged Cross," "Shalom").

Reward for the real workers   Put out carrots for Santa's reindeer as well as cookies for Santa. Write a note to Santa encouraging him to eat healthier snacks.

Tablecloth chronicles   Ask all the people at the dinner table—including scribbling babies—to write their names on the tablecloth. Embroider all the names and the date in the same color (use back stitch, French knots, or stem stitch). You and future generations will know who sat at the table each year.

B-I-N-G-O   Tell everyone to bring a wrapped white elephant. Whoever wins the round gets to choose a gift and unwrap it. The next winner can choose either that gift or another from the pile, but gifts can exchange hands only one time. The hilarity comes when people try to hold on to good gifts and rid themselves of the real eyesores. It's even more fun to watch which gifts come to the game year after year.

Make noise   Bang pots and pans at the new year. Walk out the back door, around the house, and back in the front to symbolize going out with the old and coming in with the new.

Hand-me-downs   Pass anything of special meaning to the next generation. It can be as simple as a photograph, a set of mismatched teacups, or a cake plate or as extravagant as a diamond necklace. The expense isn't the focal point; the meaning is. Be sure to include a written history of the piece. Who knows? One hundred years from now, your great-great-grandchildren may be putting out carrots for Santa's reindeer, too.

10. Acknowledge a Loss

We are healed of a suffering only by experiencing it to the full.

—Marcel Proust

Any two close friends or family members share a special set of memories. When one of them dies, many shared memories fade because the survivor loses the person most able to assist in replaying the memories. If you know someone who has lost a loved one, you can offer her a great gift: replay some of the memories with her. You'll give her a healthy opportunity to reminisce and affirm the importance of the person who meant the most to her.

The memory goes into serious rewind on "memorial days"—significant dates such as wedding anniversaries, birthdays, and the anniversary of the death. These are the days you *know* the survivor is thinking about the one who's gone. You can make the memorial days special by acknowledging that you are, too.

A Birthday Call Birthdays are times to celebrate the fact that the person entered the world—and your life has been enriched because of it. (And in the case of a parent, you *exist* because of it!) Death doesn't change that fact. If your dad were alive today, you'd be calling to wish him "Happy

Birthday." So why not call your mom to tell her you're happy he was born? Tell her some of the priceless things he taught you and how he enriched the lives of others. Ask her to tell you some of these things, too.

A Letter The one who's gone left behind a world that's different because he was here. Write a letter describing how he affected your life and the lives of others. Tell her what you miss now that he's gone.

A Visit Reminisce together. Ask her to describe some of her favorite memories. For example, if it's their wedding anniversary, have her tell you (again) all about their courtship, engagement, and wedding.

A Party We take off a whole day for a couple of old presidents. Certainly, it's appropriate for a bunch of friends to have a "We Miss Him" party in memory of someone who's gone.

11. Say I Love You

*Love doesn't make the world go 'round. Love is
what makes the ride worthwhile.*
—Franklin P. Jones

Grammatically, "I love you" is as good as it gets.
It's short: two pronouns and a verb—no messy ad-
verbs and adjectives to complicate things. It's active: the subject is doing something to the object.
It's powerful: it lists three of your favorite topics.

Creative Expressions   So stop analyzing and
say it to someone today—and every day this week.
If you want to get creative with it, try some of
these "I love you's":

• Write it on a steamy mirror (timing is important).

• Send it in a telegram.

• Fax it.

• Weave it into his tennis racket.

• Spell it in jelly beans or green M & M's.

• Write it with birdseed on his lawn.

• Give her an I Love You balloon.

- Train a parrot to say it (or buy one that already knows how).

- Carve it in balsa wood and float it in the toilet.

- Hire an airplane to pull an I Love You banner (if you see someone else's, claim it as your own).

- Shave it into the back of his hair.

- Trim it into his hedge (make sure you have the right address).

- Inscribe it on the inside of her sunglasses.

- Say it in sign language.

- Bake it into a fortune cookie.

- Brand it on his polo pony.

12. Mix It Up

If a man be gracious and courteous to strangers, it shows he is a citizen of the world, and that his heart is no island cut off from other islands, but a continent that joins to them.
—Francis Bacon

One of the golden rules of childhood is "Don't talk to strangers." It's a great rule as far as safety is concerned. Unfortunately, this stranger aversion creates a cloning device. Our peer groups are so opposite from diverse that we visit the same stores, patronize the same restaurants, watch the same TV shows, and see the same movies.

The problem with all this sameness is that it prevents you from reaching out to people who are different. If you want to make a difference in this world, you've got to mix it up with different people, different ages, different cultures, different thoughts.

Spending all your time with the same group of people severely limits your life. Your knowledge is limited because you have to rely on the information of people who have about the same amount of experience (or inexperience) as you. For example, most teenagers learn about sex from peers who aren't even sure of what they're saying!

But most important, your impact in the world is limited because your solutions show an ignorance of the big picture. If you want to shed this ignorance, you've got to step beyond the safety of your peer group and get to know some "strangers." Here are some strangers you should talk to.

Older People   Once upon a time in America, grandparents and older adults lived with the family. Children and teenagers spent lots of time with older people and learned about life from them. Nowadays, most people are separated from their grandparents by miles, busy lives, or death. So if you want to tap into the sixty or more years of knowledge and experience of the older generation, you've got to go out of your way to get them.

Get to know your older relatives. Let them expand your experience base by a few decades. Hear the dreams they had when they were young: find out what's most important to them now. Do it before it's too late.

Kids   Back in the "good old days," families were bigger, and people tended to live closer to their relatives. You couldn't help being surrounded by kids of all shapes and sizes: brothers, sisters, nephews, nieces, cousins—and a whole bunch of other kids contributed by prolific neighbors.

Nowadays, unless you work at a day-care site or do a lot of baby-sitting, you don't spend much time with kids. Which means you're missing out on certain views of life that can be seen only through the eyes of a child.

Different People   America is the great melt-
ing pot, home to people of all races, languages,
religions, and classes. Yet most of us spend our
time with people just like us. Middle-class families
befriend other middle-class families; Hispanics
identify with other Hispanics; Christians associate
with other Christians. We don't even have to *try*—it
just happens that way. We naturally seek our own
people.

How to Meet Strangers   Consider these
ideas:

- Sponsor a foreign exchange student.

- Join a swim team or basketball league on the
  other side of town.

- Try the English service of an ethnic church.

- Teach an ESL (English as a Second Language) class.

- Adopt a grandparent at a nursing home.

- Seek out the ethnic sections downtown. Try
  the foods.

- Check out the cultural section of the newspaper. Attend an event.

- Try a different brand of music—grunge for
  polka or vice versa.

- Go square dancing.

World Changers   The point is to go beyond
your comfort zone into someone else's. A word of
caution, however. Sometimes people go beyond
stepping outside their peer group; they abandon it
altogether. I see fifteen-year-olds who mix easily
with adults but are social outcasts among their
peers. Or African-Americans or Asians who despise their ethnicity. World changers tear down
walls that separate people—they don't leap over a
wall to hide on the other side.

First learn how to relate to the people around
you, then step out and get to know some strangers.

Personal Growth

13. Say a Thousand Thank-Yous

Give thanks in all circumstances, for this is God's will for you.

—Apostle Paul

In the film *Awakenings,* Robert DeNiro plays a patient who awakens in a hospital to learn that he's been in a comalike existence for *decades.* His childlike rediscovery of the outside world overwhelms him with wonder. The feel of water, a child's laughter, the taste of food—these experiences and a thousand more come crashing in on him and he's amazed. And thankful.

It shouldn't have to take a coma to awaken us to the myriad things we can be thankful for. Here's a shortcut.

Take out a sheet of paper and list things you're thankful for, from the serious to the silly and everything between: your mom, a place to live, white chocolate, big yawns, your fifth-grade teacher, computer backup files, air after a rain. You get the idea. As you write them, think of *why* you're thankful.

Set aside a few minutes each day to add to the list, numbering the items as you go along. When you get to a thousand, date the list and put it away. The next time you're feeling down, pull out the list and read through it.

Fifty Ways to Get Started

1. Family
2. Friends
3. Health
4. Ice cream
5. Sunsets
6. Laughter
7. Sounds of kitten purring
8. Chocolate—white, dark, milk
9. Church
10. Ability to read
11. Liquid soap
12. Computers
13. Puppy dog kisses
14. Chopsticks
15. Trees
16. Vistas
17. Brain that works most of the time
18. Teachers
19. Ocean
20. Paper clips
21. Greeting cards
22. Water delivery service
23. Books
24. Public library
25. Boxes and organizers
26. Ballpoint pens with caps
27. Telephones
28. Vacations
29. Unexpected letters, visits, and phone calls
30. Recyclable lunch bags
31. Rain forests

32. Zoo
33. Post-it Notes
34. Planes
35. Aspirin
36. Bible
37. House plants that are hard to kill
38. Photo albums
39. Precut carrot sticks
40. Cookie dough
41. Music
42. Cars
43. Erasers
44. Forgiveness
45. Grace
46. Key chains
47. Not wearing a tie every day
48. Summit meetings—peace talks
49. Smells of baking in the air
50. Ingredient listings on packages

Obviously, your list will differ—you may not appreciate the finer points of chocolate—but the idea is to rediscover the joy that can be found in simple things each day.

14. Lose a Habit

The unfortunate thing about the world is that good habits are so much easier to give up than bad ones.

—William Somerset Maugham

Smoking cessation patches seem like a great idea. Just stick the patch on your arm and you wean yourself from nicotine in weeks. Why not patches for other bad habits?

The gossip's patch would release a chemical that simulates the thrill of talking behind someone's back (although you'd wear it on yours). The bragger's patch would stroke your ego without your having to open your mouth—which you can't do because that's where you put the patch. Just an idea.

Until they extend the patch product line, we're left with the habit-breaking methods of old. Here are the two favorites.

Positive Reinforcement What works with dachshunds and dolphins can work with you. Set up a reward system for doing the right thing. Each time you succeed, throw yourself a treat. Here are some treat tips:

- *Don't* work solely for a distant reward that requires perfect performance.

- *Do* choose an easily and frequently administered inexpensive reward. Sometimes the praise of family, friends, and coworkers can be enough.

Aversion   That's the official name of the therapy your grade-school teacher used when she made you write something on the chalkboard one hundred times. (You probably had another name for it.) If you experience something unpleasant every time you behave a certain way, you'll begin to associate the discomfort with the behavior and curtail the behavior. Consider these simple aversion treatments:

Habit	*Treatment*
Saying "um"	Listen to a recording of your conversation, or ask others to repeat every filler word they hear you say.
Being late for meetings	Pay a quarter to each person who waits for you.
Using profanity	Keep a daily tally on a piece of paper (the trouble and embarrassment of the paperwork are unpleasant; so is the awareness of your habit).

Some habits graduate to compulsions and addictions. If your behavior has matriculated to a major-league liability, you may need the help of a professional to kick it. What a wonderful year this will become if you choose to conquer your problem. Decide to talk to someone about it today.

15. Really Read John's Book

John saw Jesus coming toward him, and said, "Behold! The Lamb of God who takes away the sin of the world!"

—Apostle John

Many folks who resolve to read the Bible cover to cover do well in Genesis, hang in there through Exodus, and bog down somewhere in the legalities of Leviticus. Another New Year's resolution lost in red tape.

Color Pictures Unfortunately, the journey ended over a thousand pages shy of one of the best parts: John's gospel. They should've just skipped to the good part.

John's telling of Jesus' life contains the most vivid word pictures in the Bible. Jesus is the bread of life, living water, the Word in flesh, a gate, a shepherd—you get the picture.

If a picture is worth a thousand words, John's gospel is an encyclopedia of good news.

16. Write a Poem

Inside every man is a poet who died young.
—Stefan Kaufer

Poetry is the art of uniting pleasure with truth.
—Samuel Johnson

Poetry can be intimidating. It's often emotional—depicting powerful meaning and images with few words. It always seems to have a deep hidden meaning—one that's arguable. Maybe you've been intimidated by poetry since the day a fellow student said, "I think this stanza depicts the emotions felt in the womb and the struggle to maintain balance between an idealistic world and a realistic world," and you thought it was a poem about flowers. That's understandable.

But poetry is just a format for discussing ordinary feelings for ordinary things. Some of the best poems ever written are very simple.

How Do You Write a Simple Poem? It doesn't have to rhyme. It doesn't have to be gushy or drippy or get you an *A* in creative writing class. Tracy Green, TV producer and occasional writer of love poems, has a simple formula.

Write the word *YOU* at the top and bottom of a piece of paper. In between, just list any words at all that come to mind when you think of the person: images, colors, moments, emotions. Don't even think about rhyme or rhythm—there's absolutely no such thing as doing this wrong. Here's an example:

YOU
delight
brilliant
quick thoughts
perfect letters
beautiful
laughter
YOU

What could possibly be more simple? Try one.

Poetry-Inciting Sources

Poetry is freedom from format. Once you start feeling comfortable, experiment with indentation, refuse to use punctuation, don't capitalize (a favorite trick of e. e. cummings), and basically feel the freedom to break grammatical rules. You'll be amazed by what you can do. You might want to start with one of these ideas:

- Scene from your window

- Your favorite animal

- What green feels like

- How air conditioning smells

- Feelings about chocolate chip cookies

- Your mom's smile

- How an angry lecture makes you feel
- Reflections
- The noise an insect makes as it flies through the air

17. Air Your Anger

Anger is a weed; hate is the tree.
—St. Augustine

Mute buttons are sneaky. The TV remote control has a mute button. With it you can turn off the sound without affecting the picture—ideal when you want to give the illusion that you're paying attention to someone and not to the show you're still following out of the corner of your eye.

Some phones have a mute button. It secretly mutes your microphone so you can talk to someone in the room while pretending to listen to the caller.

Don't Keep It to Yourself The worst place for a mute button is on a human being. On a TV or telephone, the mute is just an electrical switch. But on a human, it acts like a gag, preventing the emotions from escaping safely.

Lots of people mute their anger. Some do it consciously: when they feel the anger building inside, they press the mute button and prevent its escape. Others have put their anger on permanent mute: they don't bother with the switch anymore, so they don't even know they're angry. Either way, the anger has nowhere to go but inward. If kept in there long enough, anger can cause major damage—bitterness, numbness, depression, and isolation. Unprocessed anger becomes more corrosive with age.

If you've been operating with the mute button on, it's time to flip the switch. Start learning to express your anger with someone you can trust. You may not be able to express it to the source of your anger, but if you haven't been expressing it at all, this is a good start. You've become a pro at suppressing or repressing anger. Now you have to practice expressing it.

18 ▪ Talk to God

Before they call I will answer;
while they are still speaking I will hear.
—Isaiah 65:24

Have you ever been talking on the phone and you're in the middle of telling a story when you realize you haven't heard an "uh huh" or "really?" in the last minute or so? You start to wonder if the listener is there. Maybe she's set the phone down to turn on the TV or to make a tuna salad. Or maybe she's still there but not *there:* opening the mail, filing a nail, or drawing a mustache on the Realtor's notepad photo.

You could find out quick enough by saying something like, "Are you *listening* to me?," but you'd be hurt to know that she wasn't—and besides, you kind of like to hear yourself telling the story.

A True Listening Ear Have you ever been talking to God and wondered the same thing? Maybe He's tired of hearing about your problems and requests. Or He's bored. Maybe He has too many people talking to Him at once. He's kicking Himself for creating a round world because it means it's always time for bedtime prayers *somewhere* on the globe.

All this is silly conjecture, but it brings up a very

real question: *When you're pouring out your heart to God, is He really listening?*

If the Bible is true, the answer is yes. God knows the frustration of talking to someone who isn't listening—we do it to Him every day—so He promises again and again to listen to us whenever we call. And sometimes, if you stay quiet long enough, you can sense that He's answering.

Talk to God this week. When you call, don't worry. His phone doesn't have one of those timers. He doesn't use a stopwatch to see how long you stay on the line. Forget about the clock and talk as long as you have things to say.

19. Conquer a Fear

I believe that anyone can conquer fear by doing the things he fears to do, provided he continues to do them until he gets a record of successful experiences behind him.

—Eleanor Roosevelt

For some of us, spiders are the scariest creatures in the universe. For others, snakes cause panic. Some people are fine when it comes to creepy and crawly—it's elevators or airplanes that petrify them.

Not all fears are bad. A fear of being hit by a car while sprinting across the expressway is healthy and rational—and should keep you from sprinting across the expressway. Fear of cancer has caused many a smoker to give it up. But if your fear isn't *rational*—that is, based on strong likelihood of harm—the fear may be getting in the way of your life. If so, it's time for a conquest.

Why? Start by finding out *why* you're afraid. Lots of times we can't even remember why we're afraid of something. Take spiders. If a tarantula crawled across your three-year-old face, you have an excuse for fearing them. But chances are, you merely heard such a story or saw it on TV or had a nightmare about it after eating too much ice cream.

How? In other words, your fear is based on some pretty old data gathered when rational thinking was unsophisticated. To move past the fear, gather new data. Start by watching a spider build a web; watch how gracefully it moves. Read a book about spiders at the library. Learn how they protect you from other insects. As you see spiders in this new light, the fears based on old views will fade.

If you have a phobia that severely limits your work or pleasure—fear of flying or claustrophobia, for instance—talk to a counselor who specializes in helping people get over their fears.

20. Take a Vacation from Your Problem

The message from the moon . . . is that no problem need any longer be considered insoluble.

—Norman Cousins

Some people need to wake up and go to work on their problems. This exercise won't help them. It's intended for the folks who have been dwelling on their problems full time—to the point that they've become a part of their *life-style*. Bob is an extreme example.

Bob is the full-fledged neurotic played by Bill Murray in the comedy film *What About Bob?* Richard Dreyfuss plays Bob's psychiatrist. Desperate to give his patient something that will get him out of his hair for a week, he gives Bob a prescription. It reads, "Take a vacation from my problems."

Bob takes the prescription and discovers a remarkable thing. His problems were so much a part of him that he can't imagine surviving without them. To his surprise, his life survives and thrives without the problems.

Getting Away If your self-doubt, broken heart, loneliness, depression, or negative attitude has become a part of your life-style, take a vacation from it. Sure, you still have to go to work and fulfill your rēgular obligations. But send the rest of you on holiday: wear different clothes, listen to a different style of music, eat new foods, switch brands of toothpaste, try a new deodorant, or take a class in yodeling. Most of all, immerse yourself in activity and forswear discussing or dwelling on the problem.

Think about your vacation plans this week. Make an *un*packing list of the things you'll leave behind and an itinerary of the sights, sounds, tastes, and smells you plan to experience while you're "away." You may discover after a week or two that life without the problem is not only a nice place to visit, but you'd rather do whatever it takes to live there.

21. Be an Ordinary Hero

You may be sure that it was not for any merit that others do not possess; not for power or wisdom, at any rate. But you have been chosen, and you must therefore use such strength and heart and wits as you have.

—Gandalf to Frodo

In J. R. R. Tolkien's *The Lord of the Rings* trilogy, the Enemy seeks a ring that will give him the power to end all that's good in the world. To prevent this, the ring must be destroyed in the fires of a distant mountain. The unlikely one chosen to carry out this deadly quest is a young and harmless creature named Frodo.

When told that the future of the world depends on this mission, Frodo cries, "I do really wish to destroy it! Or, well, to have it destroyed. I am not made for perilous quests."

The Heroic Stuff We are a lot like Frodo. We wish to see an end to the bad things in this world —apathy, corruption, hatred, and violence—but we think the problems are too big and the perils too great for ordinary creatures like us. It's best that we continue to live peaceful and decent lives and leave the heroic stuff to the professional heroes—social workers, police officers, and district attorneys.

Professional heroes make a difference, but it's

not nearly enough. There's too much bad, and too few are willing to risk their comfort and safety to fight it.

The Challenge   Here's a preposterous challenge for you. Imagine that you've been chosen for a perilous quest this week. You have no idea what it will be until you're confronted with it. You'll know the quest when you see it because it will cost you something. It will clean out your wallet, make you very late for a meeting, cause you extreme discomfort, embarrass your reputation, or deprive you of precious sleep.

Before you accept this challenge, consider what you might encounter: a friend who's unemployed, has no money, and will lose the apartment if the rent isn't paid; a neighbor who's going into the hospital and needs a baby-sitter for her children for two days; a homeless person who needs a warm meal and someone to talk to; a relative you suspect is abusing his child; a policy at work that is discriminatory; a friend who's denying a real drug problem.

Are you up for this? Then live this week in search of your quest. When you find it, carry it out. If you do, there will be another waiting for you next week. As Tolkien's Gandalf said, "You have been chosen, and you must therefore use such strength and heart and wits as you have."

22. Quit Killing the Pain

*What shall assuage the unforgotten pain
And teach the unforgetful to forget?*
—Dante Gabriel Rossetti

With your first shot of Novocain, the dentist gave you an introduction to one of life's sad truths: painkillers don't heal the hurt—they just numb the pain. If the painkiller wears off before the hurt is healed, you feel it.

Science has given us an arsenal of weapons to kill physical pain, from aspirin to anesthetics. But to numb emotional pain, many of us run to age-old treatments: alcohol, drugs, sex, food, work, sleep, gambling, possessions. It's no coincidence that most of them also happen to be the most popular addictions.

The problem with these emotional painkillers is that they act as *general* anesthetics. They numb the pain, but they also numb all our emotions, dull our feelings, diminish our senses, mute our hopes and dreams, and muddle our thinking—the very things we need to heal ourselves of the pain. Instead of preventing the pain, they merely *postpone* it.

There Is Good News If you've been surviving on an emotional painkiller, there's good news and there's bad news. The bad news is that when you decide to stop anesthetizing yourself, you'll unleash all the pain you've kept tranquilized for so long. The good news is that you'll also be releasing your ability to heal the source of the pain.

There's more good news. You'll also unchain all those good things that got drugged and dulled by the painkiller: you'll have sharper senses, renewed hopes and dreams, and clearer thinking.

If you've been numbing your emotional pain instead of healing it, get on with life. Talk to someone this week about your painkiller problem; ask for help; heal the hurt.

23. Remember

Those who cannot remember the past are condemned to repeat it.

—George Santayana

Do you remember Gumby's train? The track disappeared as the train rolled over it, reappearing ahead of the locomotive. That was just fine for the show's animators—they didn't have to buy a bunch of model train track. But it was a bad deal for Gumby: the disappearing tracks left no record of where he'd been or how far he'd come.

Memories are the train tracks that show us how far we've come. They remind us of the lessons we learned. And as the epigraph above suggests, they prevent us from traveling in circles.

Rejoice in Recollections Take a look back down the tracks this week. Rejoice for the good stretches, and be thankful that the tracks didn't give out in the bad ones. Most of all, try to remember what you thought and learned from the significant moments of your past. Here are a few ways to trigger your memory:

- Flip through an old scrapbook or photo album.

- Call an old friend.

- Dig through your old record collection.
- Rent a movie you remember first seeing as a kid.
- Walk the halls of your school.
- Watch old home movies or videos.
- Reminisce with a family member.
- Read old letters and cards.
- Play a board game from childhood.
- Try to duplicate the smell of Mom's kitchen.

24 . Restore the Masterpiece

Painting is easy when you don't know how but very difficult when you do.

—Edgar Degas

Several years ago an extensive restoration of Michelangelo's work on the ceiling of the Sistine Chapel was completed. The result was extraordinary. Nearly five hundred years of dirt and dust and soot were removed without damage to the art itself, revealing color and detail no one had seen or imagined since the Renaissance.

Still, some people were critical of the restoration; they preferred the muted and aged look they had known all their lives.

The Residue You are a lot like that masterpiece: a piece of art, created by the Master, whose radiance has been obscured by the dirt and debris of life. The residue has accumulated so slowly that few have perceived much of a difference from year to year. It's difficult for even you to sense the extent of the buildup.

But the residue is real—and it has muted your colors, dulled your brilliance. It has changed the way you relate to others. You show interest but seldom excitement; you're easily amused but never amazed; you're friendly but not open; you're factual but not heart-to-heart honest.

The Removal So how do you remove the debris of life and restore the radiance of the original work? Like any art restoration, you have to figure out what features are the work of the artist and what are the result of damage and decay. In your case, that means studying the design of the Artist who created you. As you learn His design, you can see the features in you that match and those that don't. It's a lifelong restoration project.

You have one great advantage in your work. Unlike the artist who painted the Sistine Chapel, the Artist who created you is still alive, available for consultation any time. Make this a year of restoration. Ask the Master to show you what belongs to the original. Then invite Him to help you scrub away everything else.

25. Fill the Void

In the world there are only two tragedies. One is not getting what one wants and the other is getting it.

—Oscar Wilde

Have you ever bought something you've always wanted, only to have the thrill of victory shrink to a sense of emptiness when the thing didn't satisfy the void you feel inside? It's more than buyer's remorse; it's a deep longing for something you can't buy.

Seek the Spiritual If the material world cannot fill the need you have in your heart, there are two possibilities: either life is a cruel joke—a frustrating and pointless search for satisfaction you can never have—or it's a time to discover you have a spiritual side that, having been created by God, will never be satisfied until you're connected with Him.

According to Jesus (and He ought to know), "Everyone who drinks this water will be thirsty again, but whoever drinks the water I give him will never thirst. Indeed, the water I give him will become in him a spring of life welling up to eternal life."

Invite God to come and fill the void inside. He's waiting for your permission.

Wisdom

26· Make Words Count

Vigorous writing is concise. A sentence should contain no unnecessary words, a paragraph no unnecessary sentences, for the same reason that a drawing should have no unnecessary lines and a machine no unnecessary parts. This requires not that the writer make all his sentences short, or that he avoid all detail and treat his subjects only in outline, but that every word tell.

—William Strunk, Jr.

From the look of the average newspaper article, business report, or family Christmas letter, you weren't the only one who didn't fully grasp the fundamentals of writing. The average writer tangles too many words in the wrong combinations with poor punctuation, creating stuff that is a chore or a bore to read. That is what keeps her average.

If you want your words to do more than consume paper or memory bits, take a lesson from the masters of tight writing. The masters are William Strunk, Jr., and E. B. White. (Professor Strunk taught English at Cornell; E. B. White wrote *Charlotte's Web* and *Stuart Little*.) Their lesson appears in a brilliant little book called *The Elements of Style*.

If all textbooks were written like this one, television would be in big trouble. It will take you less than an hour to read this classic in brevity and wit. In that time you'll learn (or relearn) the simple rules of good writing: use the active voice; omit needless words; write with nouns and verbs; and avoid fancy words. The book presents dozens of other rules of grammar, composition, and style.

The book is short and clear because the authors make every word count. When you're finished with it, you'll want to write that way, too. Get a copy, read it in one sitting, and then keep it in your desk drawer. You'll go back to it again and again.

27. Read Something Old

The man who does not read good books has no advantage over the man who can't read them.
—Mark Twain

Most of us stopped reading classic literature when we no longer had teachers or professors forcing us to. We're haunted by the memory of those dreary classroom sessions spent searching for the DHM (Deep Hidden Meaning). Old literature seems so, well, *old*. Take Shakespeare. Why Malvolio and Marullus? What's wrong with Bert and Bob?

Actually, if you can get beyond the classroom flashbacks and the strange names, you'll probably discover why some works are called classics. Their authors may have been stuck in a certain culture and moment on the earth's timeline, but they expressed things that live in every age.

It's a pretty special moment when you discover anyone on this planet who can describe your feelings, read your thoughts, and share your quirky sense of humor—especially when this soulmate lived in a different culture, in another land, and died three hundred years ago.

Pick up a classic this week. Here are some suggestions to get you going.

Pride and Prejudice   It's the grandmother of the modern romance. Written by twenty-one-year-old Jane Austen, who found people to be hilarious, it's filled with witty conversations, kooky characters, and of course a happy ending.

A Tale of Two Cities   Its first and last lines are two of the most well known and oft quoted. It's about the French Revolution, and Charles Dickens's plot twists will keep you guessing till the very end.

Frankenstein   Nineteen-year-old Mary Shelley conceived this story during a competition with Percy Shelley and Lord Byron to see who could concoct the most horrific story. She won hands down and then wrote the novel. Be prepared to fall in love with the monster.

Cannery Row   John Steinbeck wrote this short, sad, funny tale filled with tidbits of Americana.

Put a dent in your library card and check something out.

28. Learn a New Trick

A rut is a grave with the ends knocked out.
—Frank McKinney Hubbard

Learning new tricks is at the top of the list on any child's job description. It's what kids do full time. Their repertoire of new tricks is impressive:

- Shoelace tying

- Bike riding

- Multiplication tables

- Weaseling money out of parents

- "Jump or Dive"

- Rules of baseball

- Difference between *can* and *may*

Every time they master a trick, they go on to a more difficult one. Pretty soon they're doing algebra, memorizing the unintelligible lyrics to popular songs, and perfecting the kiss. Learning new tricks is a big part of growing up.

Not for Kids Only Well, now that you're a grown-up, you spend a lot of your time trying to stay in practice with the tricks you already know: earning money, paying bills, holding on to relationships, and staying healthy. That's good, but it's still a fine idea to learn a new trick every so often—just to show yourself that you can.

A new trick can relieve stress, increase creativity, improve your mental or physical agility, and boost your ego. And it may come in handy at a dull party.

Trick List Here are a few tricks you can try:

- Juggling

- Whistling (that really loud, fingers-in-the-mouth kind)

- Walking on hands

- Signing your name backward

- Jumping rope (especially double jumps and crossovers)

- Memorizing the names of all the presidents in order

- Cutting a deck of cards with one hand

- Catching jelly beans in your mouth after flipping them up with your foot

- Riding a unicycle

- Parallel parking in a space three feet longer than your car

- Playing taps by rubbing a wet finger on the rim of a crystal glass

- Dialing your calling card number in four seconds

- Memorizing state capitals in alphabetical order

- Knowing all the answers to Trivial Pursuit questions—before the question is asked

- Eating a bowl of Jell-O without stopping for air

- Listing the *New York Times* best-sellers of the week

- Spieling off Best Pictures from the Academy —1932 to present

- Fashioning balloons into animals

- Fashioning animals into balloons

- Creating a new fashion trend

- Displaying new and unique origami techniques

- Wiggling your ears

- Making coins appear from behind people's ears

- Folding napkins into fancy figures
- Turning cartwheels
- Learning the signing alphabet

Pick a new trick and master it this week.

29. Find Out Why

Come, Watson, come! The game is afoot.
—Sherlock Holmes

Some people are paid to be inquisitive: reporters, police detectives, investigators, researchers, and spies, to name but a few. Why should they have all the fun of searching and snooping? Ask a question, then hunt down the answer. Make calls, talk to people, and look it up. The quest is as fun as the solution.

Pick One or More If you don't have any burning questions about the world around you, investigate one of these:

- Who decides the timing on the traffic signal that makes you wait so long? How are the timing and priority decided?

- How do companies print the paper on billboards? How much does it cost to rent a billboard? How many people see the sign on a given day?

- Does your social security number match a nine-digit zip code somewhere in the country? Does the government issue social security numbers according to date of birth or application, or is some other method used? Can you learn anything about a person from her number alone?

- How can different dictionary publishers claim to be "Webster's"? How does Webster feel about it? How do publishers decide which new words to put in the dictionary?

- How often do they change the population sign in your town? Who counts? How do they measure the elevation—from the sign or the city hall? Or is it an average?

30. Ask Solomon

*For wisdom will enter your heart,
and knowledge will be pleasant to your
soul.*

—King Solomon

Lots of people sound learned when you first hear them. But listen to those same words a few years, decades, or centuries later and you'll know how *wise* their words are. King Solomon's words have survived this test of wisdom for millennia.

Solomon is credited with three books of the Bible: Ecclesiastes ("To everything there is a season, a time for every purpose under heaven"); Song of Solomon (too steamy to quote here); and Proverbs —his ageless book of wisdom.

If you want to find wisdom for living, Proverbs is the book to read. Its hundreds of short proverbs deliver sound teaching in clear, understandable pieces. They're arranged into thirty-one chapters —perfect for a one-month study of wisdom. Start today.

31. Ask What If

It may be those who do most, dream most.
—Stephen Leacock

The important thing is not to stop questioning.
—Albert Einstein

If reality—*what is*—is the best it can be, there's little point in asking *what if?* You couldn't possibly imagine something better. But that certainly isn't the case. Our world is far from perfect. You can imagine one that's better and even entertain the thought of trying to get there.

A Better Life, a Better You That's the whole point of asking *what if?*: making life better. Look around you. But instead of seeing what is, ask *what if?*

- *What if* I read for thirty minutes each day with my child?

- *What if* I quit my unfulfilling job and did something meaningful?

- *What if* I stopped feeling sorry for myself?

- *What if* I continued my education to the next level?

- *What if* I wrote a book?
- *What if* I learned a foreign language?

Find a *what if* that ought to be a *what is,* then work to make it real.

32. Sleep Tight

O bed! O bed! delicious bed!
That heaven upon earth to the weary head.
—Thomas Hood

Sleep, like food, is essential to survival. How *much* sleep do you need? Everyone is different. Some people do well on five hours; others need ten or more. Thomas Edison did pretty well on four hours of sleep each night; Albert Einstein required twelve (which may explain his hair). The older you get, the less sleep you need. People in their seventies and eighties often get by on four hours because the body doesn't need to spend all night regenerating itself.

The best way to find out what you need is to experiment. Choose a wake-up time, then try going to bed at different times each night for a week. Too little sleep will make you tired and cranky. Too *much* sleep can do the same thing, so you have to shoot for the happy medium.

Some people are unconscious the moment they hit the pillow, then they sleep through cat fights and earthquakes until the alarm goes off the next morning. But most of us aren't so skilled at slumber; we need help. Here are some tips to help you sleep tight.

Unwind Your Mind   During a nonstop day, your brain doesn't have time to talk to you about anything but what you've been doing. If you go straight to bed, your mind says, "Finally! A chance to chat!" and starts telling you about who you forgot to call, what you've got to do tomorrow, and a hundred other things. Take thirty minutes to let it talk itself out.

Write It   If there are things you have to remember for the morning, write them down and forget about them till tomorrow. (A pen and pad of paper on the nightstand can help if ideas pop into your head after you hop in the sack.)

Stay Off Drugs   Caffeine, sugar, alcohol, and nicotine all interfere with sleep. For example, caffeine from coffee, tea, or cola drunk up to four hours before bed can mess with your sleep. Sleeping pills actually make sleeping more difficult when you stop taking them.

Check the Temp   Most people sleep best when the room temperature is 60° to 65° F.

Relax   Progressively relax each muscle area, starting at your toes and working slowly up to your head.

Show Your Body Who's Boss Don't go to bed until you're sleepy. If you don't fall asleep in twenty minutes, get up and don't lie down again until you're good and sleepy.

Check the Light Light can confuse and distract sleep. Make sure all windows are blocked. Even the light from a digital clock can detract from a good night of rest.

Avoid TV Although some people use it as an aid to fall asleep, it can actually make your night more restless and fragmented.

Hide the Clock People often wake in a panic and check the clock. That can develop into a frustrating habit where your body wakes each hour. Trust that the alarm will go off, and turn the clock around or hide it in a drawer.

Don't Work As much as possible, reserve your bedroom for sleeping. A room immune from the worries of the day will ensure a more restful sleep.

Mind Your Stomach A hungry or an upset stomach will drive sleep away. Drink a glass of warm milk—not because it has miraculous sleep-inducing qualities but because it tricks your stomach into believing it's full. Take an antacid if your stomach shows signs of rebelling at bed-time.

Get in a Rut   Try to go to sleep at the same time each night and get up at the same time each morning.

Social Action

33. Give It Away

Money often costs too much.
—Ralph Waldo Emerson

When Moses led the Jewish people out of slavery in Egypt, they left town too quickly to prepare provisions for themselves. It was obvious to them that everything they received from that point was a gift from God: the food they ate, the water they drank and, eventually, the land they settled in. So when they gave away a portion of their food and money, they were simply *giving back* to God what He gave them.

Many Jews and Christians continue to follow this tradition. They don't give a percentage of their money to God; *they give back a portion of what He gave to them in the first place.*

Despite this ancient tradition, most people give little or no money. For many of us, providing for needy people isn't our problem; it has become the government's job. And when the government doesn't provide food, shelter, jobs, or medical care, we declare it heartless and unfair. But a government's conscience is just an unflattering reflection of its people's. How can we expect the government to be more giving than its citizens?

If your only giving is in the form of taxes, you're missing out on a thrilling and powerful way to spend your money. Here's what happens when you give a portion of your money.

Help the People You Want   Congress decides where your tax dollars go. So the money often goes to the agencies with the right political connections or the most media coverage. By giving on your own, you ensure the survival and growth of private agencies that don't get government funds and those without headline-grabbing missions.

Feel Significant   There are over five billion people on this planet, and something inside drives us to be more than a number in the world census. We want our lives to count for something. For example, if you give money each month to sponsor a child in another country, you're paying for his food, clothing, and education.

You may not know how to program a VCR or figure out a 15 percent tip; maybe you can't touch your toes or remember which side of your car has the gas filler; but you're risking your money to keep someone else *alive*—and that's about a trillion times more impressive.

Set People Free   When you give to organizations that help needy people, you're giving others the opportunity to experience the freedom you enjoy. Most people in this world are trapped by something they can't free themselves from: hunger, disease, thirst, poverty, war, disability. People *want* to taste freedom—giving makes that possible.

Say Thanks to God If you believe that God is the ultimate provider of things, giving to others is one of the ways you can thank Him for the opportunity to use His money to meet your needs and desires. Many people take a tenth of what they have and use it to give thanks for the nine-tenths they have the privilege of using. Other people give more than that—some give nearly everything they have. (This percentage giving is also called *tithing,* from an Old English word meaning "tenth.") The joy of giving is a thrilling act of faith.

Pick a Number If you're not giving away a portion of your income, try it. First, pick a percentage. (Five percent is pretty simple for most people; 10 percent is challenging but not too overwhelming.) Then carefully choose who you want to give to. Finally, give the money. It's best to give on a regular basis (e.g., monthly) so the recipient can budget better.

Whether you give $500 or $50,000, you'll discover that your money *can* buy happiness—as soon as you give it away.

34 . Give Someone a Break

It is more blessed to give than to receive.
—Jesus

The down and out. They hold signs at intersections or buckets at supermarket entrances. Sometimes they just curl up and sleep in a doorway, under a bridge, or in the park. Wherever they hang out, they make us uncomfortable, like we should do something about their situation, like it's almost our fault. We want to help in some meaningful way, but we don't know how. So we do nothing and feel even worse.

But helping someone out doesn't have to be difficult or dangerous. Here are some ways.

Give Food Keep a few small jars of peanut butter in your car. It's full of protein and easy to eat. If you see someone who could use some food, give him a jar. Other simple handouts are trail mix, oranges, and juice packs. At a fast-food restaurant, buy an extra burger and offer it to someone who looks like she's trying to make a meal out of a cup of coffee. Say, "I bought too much food, and I hate to throw it out. Would you care to have it?"

Give Clothes Search your house for extra blankets or coats that can be given away. Take them to a shelter tonight. Put old socks, sweatshirts, and sweaters in a bag in your car. If you see someone trying to keep warm, give him something from your "warm bag."

Give Work

At home If you see someone with a "Will Work for Food" sign, "hire" him to help you clean out the garage, paint the porch, or do yard work. Feed him lunch and send him away with a generous supply of packaged food from your pantry.

At the office If you're sending out a big mailing of letters, fliers, or catalogs, have a person in need of work join the party—helping you with collating, stuffing, sealing, and stamping. Pay her a fair wage in money or the equivalent in food.

Give Money Give money each month to an organization serving homeless people in your area. Visit the project to make sure you're making a wise investment.

Give Time Volunteer at a shelter or food kitchen. You'll cook 20 gallons of chicken soup or serve 97 plates of spaghetti or wash 247 dirty dishes. Or get some friends together and make sack lunches from the leftovers in your refrigerators. Hand them out downtown.

Give Yourself Loneliness and isolation are devastating factors of street life. A few minutes of conversation—common human treatment—can mean so much to others.

Choose one of these acts of kindness, and give someone a break this week.

35. Get Angry at Evil

Hate what is evil; cling to what is good.
—Apostle Paul

Anger is okay. The problem is, most of us get angry at the unimportant things and tolerate the things that *should* make us mad. If some people got as angry about world hunger as they do about traffic jams, there'd be a lot less hungry people. And if we had as much disdain for our prejudices as we do for those of others, we'd reshape society.

Perceived Evil Take a minute to list the things you hate that probably don't deserve the energy you give them:

• Traffic

• Lines at the bank or store

• Toothpaste squeezed from the middle of the tube

• Drinking glasses left in strange places

• Litter left in your car

Genuine Evil   Now list some of the things in this world you consider most evil:

- Hunger
- Governments that block aid
- War
- Child abuse
- Planned destruction of rain forests

Fight Evil   Pick one of these genuinely evil things to be the recipient of your anger. Cross out the things on the first list as a reminder that you will redirect your disgust for them into hatred for the one big thing.

This week, when you feel anger toward one of the lesser things, think about the greater evil and what you can do to fight it. Complete the process by acting against the greater evil. In other words, do something, however small, to fight it.

36. Right a Wrong

Fairness is what justice really is.
—Justice Potter Stewart

Justice is the principle we appeal to when we cry, "That's not fair!" Based on the number of times we hear that cry, it's clear that most people have a keen sense of justice—at least as it applies to what's fair for *them*. It's *me*-justice: "*I* didn't do it! *I* don't deserve it! That's not fair for *me!*"

You-justice is not so intuitive. To judge whether something is fair for another, you have to step back and see both sides. If one side is being treated better than the other, you have injustice.

Look Take a look around you and discover an injustice. Start with the way you treat friends and family. Do you grant special favor to one child over another? Do you prejudge a friend's motives without proper evidence?

Take your search to work. If you supervise others, do you act with fairness? Injustice in the workplace goes by all sorts of names: discrimination, favoritism, backstabbing, blackballing.

Act But *finding* injustice isn't enough. You've got to right the wrong. In fact, if you find unfairness but do nothing about it, you're worse off than when you were unaware of the injustice. People may forgive your ignorance, but they'll grow to despise your indifference. In the end, either you're working to restore justice, or you are an agent of injustice.

Find something wrong this week and work to right it.

37. Stand for Something

First they came for the Jews and I did not speak out—because I was not a Jew. Then they came for the communists and I did not speak out—because I was not a communist. Then they came for the trade unionists and I did not speak out—because I was not a trade unionist. Then they came for me—and there was no one left to speak out for me.

—Pastor Niemoeller

Reconsider Conformity Let's face it. Most of us are comfortable leaving things just the way they are. We're conformists. If they handed out report cards for living, most people would get straight *C*'s:

Comfortable
Conforming
Complacent
Compliant
Calm
Cozy

There's nothing wrong with conformity. Unless . . . the crowd you're conforming to is headed the wrong way. Then it's time to stand up and say, "Something is wrong here."

Although most people seem satisfied with a *C* average in life, those who take a stand shoot for *A*'s:

Ask
Alert
Alarm
Assert
Advocate
Alive

Ask   Of all these *A*'s, the most important is *ask*.
Look at the world around you and ask, "What's
wrong with this picture?" If you do, you'll discover
distorted truth, bent rules, and glossed-over
wrongs. The sad state of our world ensures that
you'll find plenty of distortions.

You can't fix every picture. You can't fight for
every just cause. If you try, you'll spend all your
time racing from one cause to another, trying to
make a difference in all of them—and making little
difference in any of them.

Choose your battles with care. Stick with causes
your heart compels you to stand for. When other
worthy causes come along, measure their cost in
terms of how they'll affect your primary mission. If
you can't afford to fight for them, don't. Channel
the frustration of not being able to fight for these
causes into a fight you're already committed to.

Look around you. Ask, "What's wrong with this
picture?" Then stand up and make it right.

38. Go to Court

. . . that government of the people, by the people, for the people, shall not perish from the earth.

—Abraham Lincoln

In our country, the king no longer runs the show. Our government is a do-it-yourself operation now —*we* make the laws, *we* enforce the laws, *we* run the show. It's a big production, so we hire lots of people to keep it running.

One of the most interesting places to observe our operation is the courtroom. Stop by this week and see how we're doing.

Watch It Work Check out a criminal case. It will have a name like *People v. Whatshisname.* "People" refers to us—we're the ones who think Whatshisname broke one or more of our laws. To prove it, we use our own attorney. She's the district attorney or attorney general or a deputy of one of these people. "Whatshisname" is the accused—he's there to defend his innocence. He may have his own attorney to help him or use one of ours (called a public defender).

Most of the other players work for us, too. The judge is ours, but he's also the defendant's, so that makes things even. Most important, we make up the jury—the one duty we can't hire someone else to do.

The prosecutor, public defender, judge, clerk, bailiff, and jury work for us, upholding our laws. When they are just, *we* are just. When they are incompetent, unfair, or corrupt, *we* are, too. Visit a courtroom this week to make sure we're upholding the principles we declared when we said goodbye to the king.

Do Something Different Believe it or not, jury duty is a right, not a punishment. Although most people dread the mailed invitation and have a list of excuses for not attending, you have the right to be different. You don't have to wait to be called. Volunteer for duty. You'll not only flabbergast some folks, you'll be able to choose when you want to attend and you'll have a front row seat.

39. Volunteer for Something

No one is useless in this world who lightens the burdens of another.

—Charles Dickens

Once upon a time, people directly helped meet the needs of the community. Whether it was serving on the fire brigade or making meals for sick people or helping a neighbor bring in his crop, folks found needs and stepped up to fill them. In a small community the needs weren't hard to find among friends and neighbors.

This sense of community is disappearing with the small towns that fostered it. Nowadays most of us live in cities and large communities where we can remain insulated from needy people: poor people live across town, sick people are in hospitals, and older people move to a retirement community. We still help meet their needs by paying others to care for them—through taxes, insurance, and donations. But it's not the same.

Volunteering reminds you that your life counts for something. Your paid job is important, but deep down you know that if you quit, someone else will come along and fulfill the duties. As a volunteer, you're doing work that might not get done or done well if you aren't there. The world will be different —and maybe even better off—because of your presence. Two things you can give as a volunteer are time and talent.

Time   Give a few hours this week at a homeless shelter, day-care facility, health clinic, hospice, youth sports program, church, or senior center. Try it a few times; if you like it, make a time commitment and stick to it. To a nonprofit agency, a reliable volunteer is a gift from heaven.

Talent   Donate your skills to one of these agencies. If you're an artist, computer programmer, electrician, teacher, accountant, or anything else, someone out there desperately needs you. Make a list of your skills and shop around for an organization that can benefit from them.

Volunteers Wanted   Consider these ideas:

- Reshelve the books at the library.

- Start a children's story hour.

- Paint equipment at a neighborhood playground.

- Pick up litter in the park.

- Enlist students to paint a mural representing neighborhood pride.

- Teach reading to persons who have had strokes.

- Read books and magazines to blind students.

- Take food and cheer to persons who are unable to leave their homes because of illness or disability.

- Give blood.

- Organize a blood drive.

- Tutor at your neighborhood school.

- Organize a singing group at a nursing home on minor holidays (e.g., Flag Day).

- Walk dogs at the animal shelter.

- Team up groups—a children's dance school with a senior bridge club.

- Start an after-school program for latchkey children or volunteer at an existing program.

- Visit the jail.

- Raise a Canine Companion for Independence.

- Baby-sit neighborhood children once a month for tired, low-income parents.

- Run errands for an older neighbor.

Simple Living

40. Put Something in Its Place

A place for everything and everything in its place.

—Isabella Mary Beeton

There's a drawer in your house that's got some strange things in it, including an unused pocket calendar for 1987, a Garfield notepad, the microwave oven's instruction manual, an invitation to your cousin's wedding (she's already divorced), a flashlight with a burned-out bulb, a broken watch, a set of fingernail clippers, and a street map to a city you've never been to. Everyone has a drawer like this. Some of us have several.

The disorder in these drawers has an effect on us. We keep the chaos hidden (if not in a drawer, then in a closet or a cupboard or a glove compartment), but it's always there, weighing on us in subtle ways.

Clean It Out Of course, the cleanup may not be simple. The broken watch has sentimental value, and the street map *must* be worth something or you wouldn't have it, right? In fact, cleaning that drawer out will require some thought, which is why it's filled with all that stuff in the first place. You need a plan. The things in your drawer fall into four groups:

1. Things you should *keep*
2. Things you should *fix*
3. Things you can *give away* (or sell)
4. Things you can *throw away*

That's it. So make four paper signs for sorting: "Keep," "Fix," "Give Away," and "Toss." Spread out the signs and make a pile for each. Don't think too much. Just reach in the drawer, grab an object, and choose a pile. Quickness is the key here; if you pause to think, you'll bog down. Keep plucking objects out until the drawer is empty. (By the way, the pile method works for all those papers on your work desk, too. Just change the names of the piles: "File" = keep,   "Do" = fix,   "Refer" = give   away, "Trash" = toss.)

Keep Going   Now you've got four piles. Don't stop. Look through the "Toss" pile to grant any last-minute stays of execution, then throw the stuff in the trash.

Next, search the "Give Away" pile for anything you want to sell or give to someone in particular. List these errands on your to-do list; otherwise, the items will sit around the house until you get tired of looking at them and hide them back in the drawer. Put the remainder in a box to take to a thrift store.

On to the "Fix" pile. Ask yourself, Is this *really* worth fixing? If not, toss it or give it away. Each of the remaining things goes on your to-do list: take the watch to a repair shop; take the flashlight to the hardware store to find a replacement bulb.

The "Keep" pile is last. The trick with this stuff is to find the most logical place for each item and put it there. Now you're done!

Pick a drawer, cabinet, or closet to "pile" today. Do a few this week and see how the uncluttering of these small corners of your life affect your peace of mind.

41 · Dig Out of Debt

By no means run in debt: take thine own measure. Who cannot live on twenty pound a year, cannot live on forty.

—George Herbert

For most Americans, borrowing has become a way of life. The temptation is fierce. Paying with cash, you could barely afford a $150 stereo; by making monthly payments of just $30, you can own an $800 system. You would have to live in your car for a month to buy a new wardrobe (which would be pointless because you'd have no closet to hang it in), so you charge the clothing on a credit card and pay off the balance over an entire year.

The Real Cost It's seems magical. You can own things you could never afford to buy with cash. But the truth is, you don't own them. When you buy something on installment (make monthly payments), you don't really own it—the lender does. And the lender makes a killing by letting you use it. Many stores and credit cards charge you 20 percent (or more) annual interest on the money you owe them—that's *two to four times* the amount your bank is probably paying you for the use of your money.

In essence, if you have an unpaid credit card balance, you're lending your savings account to the bank so it can loan your money—*and charge you for the privilege!*

If this seems silly to you, stop! This week, begin to live by a simple rule: *don't borrow money to pay for things that go down in value.*

42. Set Aside a Sabbath

By the seventh day God had finished the work he had been doing; so on the seventh day he rested from all his work.

—Moses

Sabbath is one of God's all-time great ideas. So great, in fact, He decided to try it for Himself. If you haven't been taking a sabbath, give it a try. You'll have to do some work to make it a habit.

Different religions observe sabbath on different days. But for most of us, the issue isn't *which* day to observe it but whether we take one at all. If Sunday works for you, great. If not, choose another. (Most ministers take a sabbath on Friday or Monday. Sunday is their busiest workday.)

Get out your calendar and draw a line through each Sunday (or whatever day you choose) for the whole year. Fight to protect that day.

43. Toss the TV

I find television very educating. Every time someone turns on the set I go into the other room and read a book.

—Groucho Marx

Many otherwise normal people are doing the unthinkable: pulling the plug on television. Some are parents who don't want their children shaped by its long-term effects: increased aggressiveness, low test scores, poor eating habits, early exposure to alcohol, and so on.

Others don't like the way it absorbs their time. And a few just want to make room for a new fish tank.

Swap TV Time for . . . Whatever the reasons—and there are many—people are learning to live without the tube again. If you'd like to diminish the importance of television in your home but don't want to toss it completely, try one of these tricks this week:

- Schedule certain shows into your week and watch only those you schedule.

- Put the TV on a portable cart that stores in a closet.

- Listen to the radio instead—scan the dial for old radio dramas and comedies.

- Rediscover reading—make a Book on Tape for the Braille Institute.

- Write letters.

- Exercise your stereo—rummage through your albums, tapes, and CDs. Play all of them.

- Use TV only as a means to watch award-winning films on video.

- Discover conversation with dinner—no TV when food is served.

- Paint a picture.

- Take a class during TV hours.

- Volunteer some TV hours to a favorite charity or church.

- Develop a hobby.

- Use the time to exercise.

- Clean a closet.

- Hide the remote.

Whatever method you employ, you'll be amazed by the hours you never knew you had each day.

44. Save Childhood

You don't know what you've got till it's gone.
—Joni Mitchell

It's starting to look like Munchkin Land. Fifth graders wearing makeup, perfume, and high heels. Third graders sporting one-hundred-dollar shoes. Second graders cussing like pirates. Two-year-olds learning to spell. Why is everyone in such a hurry to spell, swear, and smell like adults?

The problem with all this early exposure to "adult" stuff is not what it gives our kids but what it *takes away*. Growing up too fast can steal from priceless pieces of childhood that kids were meant to keep all their lives. Children are simple, innocent, modest, forgiving, friendly, and unprejudiced. These childlike traits should be adult traits, too.

You may look at these traits and realize that you've already lost them. But it's not too late to get them back. To an adult, being like a child is tough. We've blocked out much of childhood, and we find it difficult to remember how we felt.

What's the Rush? As you run pell-mell at adulthood, shedding childhood as fast as you can, hurrying to look, act, smell, and talk like someone bigger than yourself, just . . . STOP: take a breath, and decide which parts of yourself to keep and which to throw away. What childlike quality are you about to toss away that you'll need to change the world?

First, here are a few things you *don't* have to do:

- Throw a tantrum in the supermarket cereal aisle.

- Streak naked through the mall.

- Go a month without bathing.

- Pick your nose during an oral report.

Then consider some things you *can* do to hold on to modesty.

Child Labor The best way to regain your childlikeness is to hang around those who still have it. Get a job at a day-care center; be a day camp counselor during the summer; volunteer as a children's coach. Spend time finding out what makes children tick: their dreams, heroes, goals, perceptions of the world, what they love and hate.

Kids' Books Reading stories that you first heard as a kid can help you remember your childhood. You'll rediscover that good children's literature is written to appeal to a child's clear and simple sense of right and wrong. In a confusing world of grays, a kid's book can help reclarify what's important.

Eyewitness Interview your parents about what you were like as a small child. Ask them to describe when they discovered certain personality traits and the significant experiences that helped shape who you are. Get out picture albums and scrapbooks. Look for old schoolwork, report cards, and souvenirs. Take a walk through your elementary school. Try to remember what was important to you, your heroes, goals, and dreams.

Let Go Let go of an "adult" behavior or habit you've developed. Stop drinking or smoking. The problem isn't that these things might make you more "grown up"—they don't. It's that they steal your *youth*.

Get Dirty Okay. Not literally but think about this: vanity is an adult trait. Little kids don't care about appearances. They laugh, cry, scream, explore nostrils, scratch behinds, and run around naked in public. They're modest—not in the reserved sense but in the unpretentious sense. They're so busy living, they don't have time to stare in the mirror.

Find Inside Friends An inside friend isn't caught up in your appearance. He cares more about what you're like on the inside. He compliments you honestly—yet isn't afraid to slip you a breath mint or point out the mustard on your face. The primary target of his compliments is your character. If you're a good listener, he tells you that. Often. If he's impressed with your honesty or sense of humor or ability to cheer people, he's not afraid to say it to your face.

Celebrate Silliness
Laughing produces higher levels of infection-fighting antibodies—it makes you feel good. On average, kids laugh up to five hundred times a day while adults laugh only fifteen times. Kids find humor in the simplest things. Recapture laughter with a list of silly things, homemade fun, and harmless practical jokes.

If you have children, nieces, nephews, or grandchildren, help them hold on to these valuable gifts. Praise and encourage them when they display these characteristics. Set an example by holding on to them.

45 . Show Your Wallet Who's Boss

The problem with money is that it makes you do things you don't want to do.

—*Wall Street*

If you're looking for money advice these days, you're in luck. Hundreds of books, dozens of newsletters, and several magazines are devoted to the topic. Or you can tap into the genius of money managers via computer, TV, or telephone 800 lines. Any one of these sources can tell you all about money market accounts, zero coupon bonds, and closed end mutual funds.

Of course, none of this investment advice will do you much good if you never have any money to invest. Which means money management has to start with your wallet—it's the biggest money loser you've got. Here are some tips to help you get control of your spending; try some of them this week.

Ask Why Ask, Why do I want to buy this thing? It's amazing how silly some of your purchases seem when you ask that question.

Wait a Week   A waiting period gives you time to consider whether you really want the item. Do this for purchases over a certain dollar amount, such as twenty or fifty dollars.

Don't "Save Money" by Spending It
Walk away when someone says that a deal is "too good to pass up" or that "you'll never find as good a deal as this one." You will *always* find a better deal. Keeping your money in savings is a better deal. Don't let salespeople pressure you into making decisions "before it's too late." If you shop around, you'll usually find something as good or better—or discover you didn't need the thing after all.

Shop with People Who Spend Less   If you shop with big spenders, chances are, you're going to spend more money than you should.

Write It Down   Every time you spend money, write down what you bought and how much you paid. Buying something isn't as easy when you have to find your expense book and write down the transaction. Hold a contest with yourself to see how little money you can live on each week. Set goals and reward yourself when you meet them.

Get Some Advisers   If your spending problems are serious, ask a friend to hold you accountable. Make a promise to consult him before spending more than fifty dollars on any one thing.

46. Take the Long Way

To travel hopefully is a better thing than to arrive.

—Robert Louis Stevenson

Ants are all business, no pleasure. They move with great purpose, lugging huge chunks of stuff here and there, bumping into each other and hardly stopping to apologize. They're not big on sightseeing; they've got work to do, and it's straight there and straight back and all over again.

Most of us are a lot like ants. Whether it's a drive from work or a walk to the market, we charge off with only the destination in mind and don't stop until we get there. We have straight sidewalks and superhighways and synchronized traffic signals, all designed to get us straight to where we're going with minimum interference. But something's missing.

Detour The next time you go somewhere, take the long way. You'll discover things you've never seen before, turning a routine trip into a sightseeing experience. You'll get a new perspective, maybe even trigger an idea that leads to international fame or outrageous wealth or a Nobel Prize —or maybe just a keen paper towel dispenser design. (And if you're a big-time government official, you'll frustrate any mean schemes planned against you by the bad guys.)

When you choose your detour, don't go berserk and drive through Belize on your way to work (unless, of course, Belize isn't too far away). Just get off one exit early or turn the other direction when you leave home.

Long Ways   Here are a few journeys you can take:

- Drive the speed limit.

- Take surface streets instead of the freeway.

- Park your car a mile from your destination and walk.

- Take the smallest streets.

- Try public transportation.

- Bike one day a week.

- Try to see one sunrise and one sunset on the same workday at your home.

- Stop somewhere that catches your eye.

- Stop somewhere you've been "meaning" to stop for years.

- Turn right at stop*lights,* left at stop *signs*— see where you end up.

47. Unload Excess Stuff

You don't see no hearses with luggage racks.
—Don Henley

The first time you moved away from home, you didn't own much. Maybe you filled a suitcase or two and a few cardboard boxes with trophies and photo albums and your music collection.

Your next move was tougher. You had to borrow a friend's pickup to carry everything, including those nifty shelves you made from boards and bricks, plus the junk your roommate left behind when he moved out in the middle of the night without paying rent. A few moves and several roommates later, you're renting a U-Haul truck and bribing strong-backed friends with pizza and promises that you'll return the favor on their next move.

Stuff and More Stuff Now you've reached the point where they won't rent you a truck big enough to move all your stuff because you're not licensed to drive a semitrailer rig. So you hire a moving company. As you're boxing up your fifty-third carton of possessions, you ask yourself, Do I really need to own all this stuff? Sure, you have the necessities: toothbrush, blanket, the Green Bay Packers pajamas. Many possessions are *almost* essential: tools, toaster oven, couch, the Hits of the

Seventies CD collection. But there are several hundred pounds of pure luxury—two stereos, three televisions, five space-age kitchen appliances, and enough clothes to outfit a family of twenty-seven.

Part of you says there's nothing wrong with owning all this stuff—it makes life easier and more enjoyable. But another part of you (including your lower back) questions whether you might be happier with less: less clutter, fewer headaches, lower costs for fixing and mending (something is *always* breaking), and less worry about stuff being stolen.

Lose the Load   Here's an idea. Get rid of it. Not all of it—just the stuff you really can't think of a compelling reason to hold on to. Go through the closets and cabinets, shelves and cupboards, looking for anything that isn't essential. With each suspect item, ask yourself this question: Would my life be worse off without it?

If the answer is no, put it in a discard pile. Now pack it up and deliver it to the Salvation Army, Goodwill, or another organization that can benefit from selling it. (Important safety tip: if you're married, make sure your spouse has a chance to veto your decisions—or you may find yourself back at the thrift store, buying back your possessions.)

Peace of mind is a timid possession, disappearing as things get crowded. If you want more of it, cut back on less-valuable possessions.

48. Stop the Stockpile

Shed your extra clothing
Keep your baggage light
Long will be the battle
Tough will be the fight

—Anonymous

As kids, we didn't worry much about stockpiling our possessions: we grew out of clothes and broke toys faster than our parents could buy new ones, so closet space was generally available. Well, we've stopped growing (vertically, anyway), and we're a little gentler on our "toys" now that we pay for them ourselves, so our closets are filling up with new stuff but we're not unloading the old. We're stockpiling.

A New Policy If your world is filling up with stuff, establish a nonaccumulation policy. Here's how it works. Whenever you want to buy something new, you have to get rid of something like it. If you want a new shirt, you go to your closet and pick out a shirt to give away. A pair of new shoes costs one pair of old shoes given to Goodwill. Birthdays and Christmas can be tough because you may get lots of clothes as gifts and have to give away as many items.

Of course, you can have exclusions in the policy. Socks and underwear, for example. A single male can go without doing laundry for precisely as

many days as he has pairs of socks and underwear. Conclusion? You can never have enough
socks and underwear. If you collect something as a
hobby, the collection is excluded. So are keep-
sakes and personal papers. And if you need things
for your work—tools, books, office equipment—
you may wish to hang on to what you already have.
The rest of your stuff can fit in the policy: clothes,
shoes, jewelry, sports equipment, stereo equipment, and whatever else you might have a tendency to stockpile.

The Payoff The biggest payoff with a nonaccumulation policy isn't what it does to your storage
space but how it changes your values. Your buying
habits will change—getting a new toy will cost you
money, and it'll cost you an old toy you like as
much. It also compels you to attach the act of giving to the act of receiving. If you *want* something,
you must *give* something. Not a bad connection.

Put the policy into effect this week by giving
away items in exchange for the things you've ac-
quired in the past two months.

49. Go to Recess

In every real man a child is hidden that wants to play.

—Friedrich Nietzsche

Our grade-school teachers had it figured out. We were more fun and attentive after we had a break from our studies. Too bad they're not around to enforce recess for grown-ups.

A break is a productivity tool. Whether you're finger painting or figuring out a million-dollar deal, you'll do it better after a break. A break will relieve tension—especially when the tension is deadline related.

A break can also relieve your *at*tention. The mind is a versatile athlete, capable of both sprints (moments of high concentration) and marathons (long, steady thought). But it doesn't perform well when you try to sprint a marathon. Give it some attention breaks. (TV programmers understand this; it's the reason they spend lots of money on programming bits to insert between the commercials.)

Here are a few tension- and attention-relieving recesses for grown-ups.

Zag You can't zigzag if all you do is zig. If you sit at a desk all day, stand and walk around. If you're on your feet all the time, lie down. It's that simple.

Move Around   Tetherball and foursquare may not be appropriate, but a few sit-ups, push-ups, or stretching exercises might be. Five minutes of physical work can burn away a lot of mental strain.

Snack   The candy commercials have a point. Low blood sugar can lower your ability to think. A quick snack can give you a temporary boost until a real meal.

Read   A few minutes in a good book can take you thousands of miles and hundreds of years away from your work—and have you back in business as soon as you close the cover.

Play   Pull up a computer game or jump into a crossword puzzle. Mind games demand enough attention to get your mind away from your work without taxing it too much.

Work   When you can't take a full break, at least take a recess from the *kind* of work you've been doing. If you've just spent the past two hours inching your way through a colossal spreadsheet, take fifteen minutes to return some calls. If you've been on the phone for a solid hour, write a letter.

Nap   Some people can benefit from catnaps as short as five minutes. Try this: lie on your back and prop an outstretched arm on a thick book. Hold a set of keys in your outstretched hand. Let yourself fall asleep. Within a few minutes your hand will relax; the keys will drop and wake you.

With no school bell to tell you when to go to recess, you'll have to create your own reminders. Set a watch to beep each hour or use an alarm clock. Schedule breaks into your work this week.

50. Deny Yourself

Just say "NO!"

—DARE

Acts of discipline are mental photographs; they provide you with evidence of your ability to make difficult choices. When things get tough—when it seems that your goal is to change the unchangeable, beat the invincible, do the impossible—you can look back at the pictures of your past accomplishments and know that you've been to this point before and won. Every act of discipline prepares you for greater challenges ahead.

Meet the Challenge Fill your mental photo album with evidence of your growth and increased ability. Push yourself with creative weeklong challenges. At the end of the week, take on a new challenge. Here are weekly challenge ideas:

- Get around without a car.

- Go without sugar, meat, coffee, or something else you love.

- Read a Bible chapter each morning.

- See every sunrise.

- Memorize a great quote each day.

- Walk two miles every day at noon.

- Do fifty push-ups a day.

- Invent a new recipe each night.

Don't Compare Warning: if reading a list like this overwhelms you with guilt and you resolve to accomplish all these things immediately, STOP. Discipline doesn't work that way—it's not a competitive sport. Comparing yourself to these examples—or anyone else's—won't make you more disciplined. You will always find people who are much more disciplined than you. Next to them, you're an undisciplined failure. On the other hand, you don't have to look far to find people who *never* reach for new challenges. Compared to them, you're a pillar of discipline.

Your only true competition is the voice inside that says, "You can't do it—give up." Every act of discipline becomes a self-portrait—a picture of you winning.

51. Throw Away the Scale

Obesity is really widespread.
—Joseph O. Kern II

How on earth did people worry about their weight before the invention of the bathroom scale? They didn't. They knew that being fit is a matter of how you look and feel—not how much pressure your body applies to the floor.

Measuring your fitness with a scale is silly. Aerobic exercise—the best way to burn fat—adds muscle to your body as it burns fat calories. Burning five pounds of fat may add three pounds of muscle. That's *eight pounds* of good news: five pounds of lethargy are now gone, and three pounds of good-looking strength and energy have arrived. But to the scale, you've made just *two pounds* of progress.

Quit trying to impress the scale. If you want to be trimmer and feel better about yourself, eat smart and exercise right.

Eat Smart You don't have to be a biochemist to figure out the right foods to eat. Your body shouts out the answers. Smart food makes you feel light and alert and satisfied. Greasy, fatty, or sugary food makes you feel heavy and a little sick in the stomach.

Avoid gimmick diets, especially those that severely restrict your intake. When your body senses a shortage of food, it downshifts into an energy-conserving lower metabolism rate—which means it's burning your fat more slowly. When you break the fast, the body takes its time increasing the metabolism. The result? Your body can't burn the new shipment of calories fast enough, so it tucks them away for safekeeping. In other words, you create more fat. It's a senseless cycle.

Exercise Right Any exercise will do you good, but only certain kinds shift your body into a serious fat-burning mode. Low-intensity aerobic exercise is best: brisk walking, bicycling, running, and swimming. The fat-burning part kicks in about twenty minutes into the exercise. Until then, your body burns glycogen, a nonfatty fuel that's already stored in the muscles. (This is the instant fuel we humans have used for everything from outrunning dinosaurs to making a tight airline connection.) So if you jog for twenty-five minutes, you're burning fat for just five minutes—not enough to matter. You'll burn the fat a lot faster if you spend at least forty-five minutes to an hour in a low-intensity exercise.

It seems like a *high*-intensity workout—sprinting or jumping rope, for example—would burn the fat quicker. Actually, the reverse is true. That's because when your muscles are really pumping, they need good fuel in a hurry. Instead of switching to fat after twenty minutes, you keep burning glycogen. (When a runner "hits the wall," she's referring to that awful moment when the glycogen runs out and she has to use less-efficient fuel stored in the body.)

If you eat smart and get three sessions of aerobic exercise a week, you'll see and feel differences no bathroom scale can measure.

52. Save a Life

How long would we remain free in a daily, desperate, overpopulated scramble for bread?
—David Brinkley

The ideas in this book can help you make this year your best ever. This last idea will allow you to make it the best year ever for someone you don't even know . . . yet.

You can do this through child sponsorship. Organizations such as Compassion International can link you with a child in another part of the planet who needs help to survive. For about twenty-four dollars a month you can help provide school, skill, sustenance, and spiritual guidance. You can write letters back and forth to stay informed on your child's progress.

Education Your money changes other lives, too. It benefits the child's family, so brothers and sisters are helped (Third World families tend to be large). Some of your money goes to the kid's school, which uses it to hire and train teachers, buy books and equipment, and deliver a better education to all its students.

Understanding Your personal horizons will broaden. You—and the child you sponsor—will gain a better understanding of what life is like for someone else as you correspond.

Hope Most of all, your money provides hope and vision and purpose to a child who will grow up to become a leader in her community and country. In the end it's not money or programs that transform countries—it's people. Your sponsored child will be one of those people.

If you'd like to sponsor a child, photocopy or tear out the form on the next page and send it to

Compassion International
P.O. Box 7000
Colorado Springs, CO 80933
1-800-336-7676

How to Make Each Year Better for a Child in Need

☐ Yes! I want to help make each year better than the last for a child who needs me.

I prefer to sponsor ☐ a boy ☐ a girl ☐ either one

From ☐ any country ☐ Africa ☐ Asia
☐ Latin America ☐ Caribbean

Please select a child for my consideration and send me his or her photo, case history, and complete sponsorship packet.

If I wish to begin immediately, I will enclose my first sponsorship check, indicating the amount here:

☐ $24 (one month) ☐ $72 (three months)

Name _____

Address _____

City _____ State _____ Zip _____

Phone (_____)_____

Sponsorship is tax deductible and receipts will be sent.

COMPASSION
INTERNATIONAL
P.O. Box 7000
Colorado Springs, CO 80933
1-800-336-7676

52
WAYS TO
REDUCE
STRESS
IN YOUR LIFE

52
WAYS TO
REDUCE
STRESS
IN YOUR LIFE

Connie Neal

OLIVER
NELSON

Thomas Nelson Publishers
Nashville

Published in Nashville, Tennessee, by Oliver-Nelson Books, a division of Thomas Nelson, Inc., Publishers, and distributed in Canada by Word Communications, Ltd., Richmond, British Columbia.

The Bible version used in this publication is THE NEW KING JAMES VERSION. Copyright © 1979, 1980, 1982, Thomas Nelson, Inc., Publishers.

Printed in the United States of America.

ISBN 0-8407-9653-6

✳ Contents

✳ Introduction

Life is stressful. You may think of stress as something you want to eliminate from your life. Actually, it is stress overload that is harmful. Research studies show that having too little stress can be as hazardous to your health as having too much stress. Stress occurs whenever there is a life change upsetting your equilibrium. Your whole being (body, mind, and emotions) reacts to the change by preparing you to protect yourself in the new situation. You benefit from a manageable degree of stress by responding to the changes in life.

The key to a healthy life is to find balance so that your level of daily stress is stimulating but manageable. Therefore, your goal is to reduce stress to a manageable level and manage the stress you cannot eliminate. This book is full of ideas to help you manage daily stress in healthy ways.

A Framework of Understanding Before you go on, here is some basic information about stress that gives you a framework to work from. With this understanding, you can choose which ideas in this book would best help you manage daily stress.

Stress occurs whenever a real event or perceived danger upsets your psychological and/or physiological equilibrium. In this way, human beings are similar to animals in the wild. A deer who hears approaching footsteps will immediately react in preparation for a life-preserving escape. This type of physical reaction is similar to a person who senses danger and responds physically in a way that makes her able to survive. For example, you are driving, and another car swerves into your lane. Immediately, your body responds to the stress in a way that allows you to react quickly and get yourself out of danger. This stress reaction is helpful to you.

However, human beings are not merely animals, responding to physical happenings. A human being also reacts to conceptual dangers. Here are some examples of conceptual dangers that may cause a stress reaction:

- Fearing that a crime may be committed against you

- Worrying over the state of the environment and world affairs

- Thinking of all your pressing commitments over the next month and worrying that you may fail to meet them all

- Fretting because you don't know how you will financially make ends meet

- Preparing for a major holiday or special event

- Preparing for a test and considering how the results will affect your future

In each of these examples, there need not be any actual danger or threat to cause a stress reaction. The perceived or anticipated threats are enough to create stress. Even though these conceptual dangers may never occur, you can experience stress by the way you think about what could happen. You respond to what you believe to be real, just as though it were real.

When stress occurs, whether from good or bad circumstances, you will react physically, emotionally, and behaviorally. Your body responds to stress with a fight or flight reaction. The involuntary physical reactions include muscle tension, a racing heart beat, and a surge of adrenaline that brings you into a state of alertness. Emotionally, you may become irritable, depressed, and so on. Stress may affect your behavior by creating distractions that keep you from functioning up to par. You may change your response to others, increase or decrease your activity, and so on.

Psychologists say that most people have an adaptive range capable of responding to the ups and downs of everyday life in healthy ways. However, in our modern world, change takes place at an amazing rate. Each stressful stimulus calls for a response, demanding that you process information and make decisions about what this means to you and what you should do about it. Conflicts, time demands, and problems may arise faster than you can reasonably deal with them. The stressors of modern life can accumulate to a state of stress overload, which taxes body, mind, and spirit.

Medical studies have shown that living in a constant state of stress overload can undermine physical well-being. People who live with high stress levels make more mistakes, have more accidents, get sick more often, and experience higher rates of depression and physical pain than others who are able to reduce or manage stress well. Therefore, you would do well to identify what may be causing stress overload in your life and take action to reduce stress to manageable levels. If some of the stressors in your life are realities you cannot change, you can still learn to manage stress in healthier ways.

Since you are trying to keep a healthy balance, you may benefit from having a gauge by which to measure the level of stress in your life. This objective scale may also help you design an overall strategy for coping with the stress factors you face and cannot change immediately.

A Stress Gauge The "Social Readjustment Rating Scale" is used to measure the relative impact of common life changes. It was published in 1969 by psychiatrists Thomas H. Holmes and Richard Rahe. This scale includes both good and bad experiences known to cause a stress reaction. The scale uses a measure of life change units (LCU) to rank common life experiences in order of their stressful impact. According to this scale, the death of a spouse ranks highest at 100 LCU; divorce ranks at 73; even a happy occasion such as marriage ranks at 50; and an outstanding personal achievement ranks at 28. At the lower end of the scale, vacation and Christmas rank at 13 and 12 respectively, while minor violations of the law rank at 11. In Holmes and Rahe's study, whenever the cumulative life change units reached more than 200, subjects began to suffer from physical ailments associated with high levels of stress.

Everyone experiences stress. The trick is to keep the level manageable by limiting stress overload and learning to use stress to your advantage. This book presents 52 ways to reduce stress, manage stress, and limit the negative effects of stress overload.

1 ✳ Exercise Regularly

Exercise is known to reduce stress and relieve tension. Studies indicate that exercise reduces feelings of anxiety, depression, and hostility associated with high levels of stress. There are physiological explanations for these positive effects of exercise. When you experience stress, your body produces a potentially toxic hormone, noradrenaline. Exercise helps burn off noradrenaline. Exercising also releases endorphins, which are naturally produced painkillers; they elevate your mood and help you relax both physically and psychologically. Medical research has confirmed that exercise alleviates muscle tension better than tranquilizers. So, exercise is a great way to work off the negative effects of stress and release the tension.

Physical fitness also prepares you to handle stressful situations better. University studies have shown that people who are physically fit can handle stress without succumbing as readily to illness or depression. If you are in the midst of stressful circumstances that you don't have the power to change, staying in good physical condition minimizes the negative effects of stress on your physical health.

Here are some ways you can plan to use exercise to reduce daily stress.

Give Yourself Recess Plan your schedule to integrate exercise into your routine demands. If work is stressful, plan to exercise during your breaks or at lunchtime. If you have time and opportunity, work out at a gym or take a swim during, before, or immediately after a stressful workday. If time and exercise facilities are not available, take a brisk walk around the block, climb stairs in your building, or innovate another way to exercise where you are.

If you can make your exercise break fun, that is even better. Playing while exercising gives you the physical effect and can take your mind off matters that may contribute to psychological stressors.

Exercise Regularly To have the best effect in stress management and reduction, maintain an exercise routine. Plan to exercise three times each week for at least twenty minutes. Choose an activity you enjoy or something you can do with a partner so you will be motivated to continue long term.

Don't Exercise in Stressful Ways Identify the exercise situations that stress you out, and choose other options. For example, if the thought of being seen in a swimsuit makes you uncomfortable, swimming in a public place will not have the stress-reducing effect you seek. If you are so competitive that team sports create as much stress as you burn off from the physical exercise, find an individual sport you enjoy.

Exercise to Music Combine the tension-relieving effects of exercise with the uplifting effects of your favorite music. Choose an exercise class where the instructor's taste in music matches your own. Listen to tapes on a portable tape player while you exercise alone. View aerobic exercise videos with tunes that meet your musical tastes.

Exercise Rather Than Take a Nap Exercising can actually increase your energy level and make you feel more refreshed than being physically inactive. The next time you feel like collapsing after a stressful day, try taking a brisk walk before you lie down for a nap. If you still feel like taking a nap after your walk, do so. However, you may be surprised to find that the exercise invigorated you and relieved your fatigue.

Don't Overdo a New Exercise Routine Be careful not to wear yourself out or injure yourself starting a new program that is too strenuous. Instead, start gradually with a noncompetitive aerobic activity, such as brisk walking, swimming, or jogging. Then gradually adjust to a more demanding exercise routine.

2 ✳ Face Problems with a Positive Attitude

The negative effects of stress arise from perceiving situations as being threatening or potentially harmful. Therefore, it is not necessarily what you experience directly but what you believe about the meaning of your experience that creates stress.

For example, if your child is late coming home from school and you believe he has been hurt, you will experience a stress reaction. When he comes in the door and reminds you that he had an after-school activity, your heart stops racing, and you breathe a sigh of relief. However, your tension level and your physical reaction were the same *as if* your child had been hurt. Your body has undergone a stress reaction. On the other hand, if your child is late coming home from school and you assume she is okay, your body will not have a stress reaction.

Be Optimistic Psychological studies confirm that optimists suffer fewer physical signs of stress than pessimists. That is easily understandable. Your predisposition toward optimism or pessimism will determine how many unnecessary stress reactions you experience in your lifetime. If you are in a constant state of turmoil because of anticipated disasters that never arise, your body goes through the stress reaction just as though the disasters were realities.

Your mental attitude toward life will also have an effect on how many stressful situations you encounter in real circumstances. If you don't think you have the ability to change your life for the better, you will be more resigned to allowing yourself to be a victim. Therefore, you may remain in situations where you are in constant danger. If you are an optimist who believes you can make a difference in the world, you will not simply accept difficult circumstances. You will identify problems and devise a plan to solve the problems creating stress in your life.

Here are some ideas for nurturing a positive attitude and avoiding unnecessary stress.

Think First When you begin to have a stress reaction, stop to ask yourself if you are reacting to what is really happening or what you fear may have happened. If you are responding to a catastrophe that may not have occurred, offer your mind some alternative possibilities of what may have happened. Let's go back to the example of the child being late from school. Suggest to yourself that he may have stayed to help the teacher, he may have detention, he may have told you of after-school activities that you forgot, and so on. Considering a list of possible realities will keep you from assuming the worst. As you check out each possibility, you can focus your mind on the task at hand and postpone a full stress reaction until you know whether one is warranted.

Don't Jump to Conclusions   When an obstacle or a problem presents itself, look for solutions rather than consequences. If you catch yourself saying, "Oh, no! Now something terrible will happen," stop yourself before you jump to conclusions. Ask yourself, What can I do to counteract this obstacle? What can I do to prevent something terrible from happening? Focus your attention on doing whatever you can to remedy a problem before resigning yourself to despair.

Learn from Others   Listen to motivational tapes and read motivational materials. You can learn optimism. You can develop a more positive attitude toward life. If you are not typically optimistic, study the instruction of people who practice seeing life from a positive perspective.

3 ✱ Tense and Relax Your Muscles

Stress triggers a set of biochemical responses. Physical relaxation triggers a set of biochemical responses that are practically opposite of those caused by stress. By tensing and relaxing your muscles, you can counteract the physical effects of stress. It may also help reduce tension headaches, migraines, anxiety, hypertension, and other stress-related physical symptoms. Some people find that tensing and relaxing the muscles throughout the body even helps them go to sleep at night by relieving the accumulated physical tension of the day.

Here is how to tense and relax your muscles to relieve stress:

- Find a room where you can relax without interruption and a time when you will not be disturbed.

- Remove your shoes and wear comfortable, loose-fitting clothing.

- Lie face up, eyes closed, with your arms comfortably at your sides. Place your palms upward.

- Breathe slowly and deeply.

- Starting from the top of your body, tighten all the muscles in your head and face (including your tongue) as much as you can. Hold for a count of five, and then relax as completely as you can.

- Take a slow, deep breath before moving to the neck and shoulder muscles. Repeat this tightening, relaxing, deep-breathing process as you focus on each part of your body: arms and hands, chest, abdomen and buttocks, legs, and feet and toes. Remember to hold each tension pose for a count of five. After tensing each muscle group, relax thoroughly and breathe deeply.

After you have finished, return to your normal activities. You should feel relaxed and refreshed. You might want to use this process whenever you take time out to relieve stress during the day. You'll learn about taking time out in the next chapter.

4 ✳ Take Time Out

Whenever you realize stress is getting to you, take time out. If you don't, the stress caused by one situation will carry over into the next and will be compounded. So excuse yourself for a few moments. This allows you to regain your composure and to take specific steps for relieving the stress before adding more.

Here is an example. You arrive home from a stressful day at the office. Your children are eager for your attention, and your spouse greets you with a list of important concerns that require decisions on your part. If you do not first take time out to unwind from the demands of the day, you might be irritable and short-tempered with your family.

However, in most cases you can simply explain to your family that you need thirty minutes alone before you tend to their needs. Then take that time to put the day's concerns to rest and to do something relaxing. Take a bath, listen to music, walk around the block, or read something for pleasure. After your time out, you will be better able to relate to others and to do what you need to do.

This is also a good practice to use with children who are overwhelmed by schoolwork or other demands on their time. If you notice that your children seem stressed, suggest that they take time out from homework or whatever is causing the stress. Then help them engage in a fun, relaxing activity for a while. When they resume their work, they will be better able to cope without being overwhelmed by stress.

5 ✳ Resolve Ongoing Conflicts

Ongoing conflict makes for great drama in plays, novels, or adventure movies because conflict causes tension. In any story, once the conflicts are resolved, the tension is lost, and the story must soon come to an end or lose reader interest. In your personal life the stress of ongoing conflict creates ongoing tension. If you want to resolve the continual tension, you must attend to resolving ongoing conflicts.

Stress is the perception of danger or a reaction to changing circumstances that may threaten you. Conflict creates stress because you must fight to win an ongoing battle. If you have internal conflicts that are unresolved, you must continually battle against yourself. If ongoing conflicts are a part of your relationships at home or work, you must live on the defensive. You must always be on the alert to what might happen if the person opposing you should get the upper hand. Therefore, you learn to live on the alert. This continual stress—added to whatever stress occurs with the normal ups and downs of life—can become overwhelming.

Whether the ongoing conflicts are internal or external, at home or at work, resolving them will significantly reduce daily stress. Here are some ideas about how you can resolve ongoing conflicts.

Get Professional Help   If you have tried to resolve ongoing conflict on your own without success, consult a professional counselor or therapist. A trained counselor can often help you see things from a new perspective, and as a result, you can find new ways to deal with internal conflicts and conflicts in relationships with others.

Choose a counselor who has a good reputation for helping resolve the kind of conflict you are facing. You may want to consider a member of the clergy, a marriage and family counselor, a substance abuse counselor, an employment counselor, or another professional who inspires trust in your particular situation.

Change Your Circumstances   Physically move away from someone with whom you have an ongoing conflict. For example, if you constantly clash with someone in your office, see if you can move your work space away from the person's presence.

Change your schedule. If you can, adjust your schedule so you don't have to spend more time than is absolutely necessary with a person with whom you are in conflict.

Change Your Relationship   Try to make friends with the person. Show gestures of kindness and genuine interest in the person's welfare. Ask questions that will help you understand what puts you at odds with the individual.

Agree to disagree on issues where you are poles apart. End the relationship if necessary.

6 ✻ Get Enough Rest

Rest is vital to maintaining general good health and being able to handle stress. However, often it is a challenge to get enough rest when you are stressed because stressful situations may disturb your ability to rest.

You must make choices that help you get enough rest, even if that is a challenge. Rest is so important to well-being that God included a command to rest in the Ten Commandments. Perhaps if getting enough rest was something we were inclined to do automatically, God wouldn't have made it a command.

You can choose to get enough rest. Here are some tips to help you.

Rest from Your Work Plan to give yourself at least one day each week when you don't do any work. Make this a day when you are not on call, when you are not thinking about pressing deadlines and duties. Give yourself time out from your work responsibilities. That may take careful planning. If you know that staying home means you will be drawn to your desk or briefcase, plan an outing far away from telephones, fax machines, and opportunities to work.

Rest by Sleeping You need your sleep. When you sleep, your brain replenishes essential biochemicals, which help you cope with stress. Any new parent can testify to the effects of a lack of sleep combined with a stressful situation. Even though stress can cause sleep difficulties, take the following steps to make sure you get enough rest:

- Establish a regular sleeping and waking schedule.

- Don't drink anything containing caffeine in the four hours preceding bedtime.

- Cut back on vigorous physical or mental activities before bed. Instead, try some light exercise several hours before bed, followed by more subdued activities that tend to calm you (such as reading, listening to music, and so on).

- If you have trouble falling asleep, get up and do something relaxing, such as having a warm glass of milk, reading a lighthearted novel, watching a pleasant movie, or listening to soothing music. Don't get up to do something that stirs up worries, such as working. Go back to bed when you feel sleepy.

Rest Periodically Give yourself periods of regularly scheduled rest. One hour a day, do a relaxing activity you enjoy. One day a week, concentrate on restful scenarios. Take regularly planned vacations each year.

Take a Break from Tension-Filled Environments

Rest by occasionally removing yourself from environments where demands are being made of you and expectations are placed on you. If a particular place is too tension filled for you, take a break by removing yourself from there for a time until you are able to regain your composure.

Rest from the Bombardment of External Stimuli

Set aside periods of time where you cut out all the noise, turn off the television, ignore news reports, and get away from all the information coming at you. When you relieve yourself of all the external stimuli, you will be better able to get in touch with what is going on inside you. Sometimes internal stresses mount because you are so caught up in the flurry of all that is happening around you that you aren't able to address your inner needs.

7 ✳ Give Yourself Enough Time

Time pressures contribute heavily to the experience of stress in our culture. In days gone by, most people could easily cut themselves some slack in terms of time demands. Life in an agricultural-based economy flowed in seasons, which allowed room for a person to compensate for stress. Life in today's age of instant information flies by in split seconds. Microwave meals, instant coffee, fast food, "Headline News," fax machines, overnight delivery services, supersonic transport—all of these timesaving devices create expectations of having what we want and having it *now* if not sooner. However, this high-speed lifestyle also means that others expect what they want of us *now* if not sooner.

These changes in technology have caused society to change, reflecting the demand to have things instantaneously. Instead of using the time saved by these innovations to enjoy more relaxation, we have raised the demands of what we expect ourselves to accomplish. In our culture, both home and workplace seem characterized by a sense of urgency, an unrelenting pace, immediate deadlines, and overcommitment.

Make a Choice You have a choice to make. You can choose to race to keep up with our fast-paced culture, or you can choose to use timesaving devices to give yourself more time. If you choose to do so, you can give yourself more discretionary time instead of placing higher demands on yourself just because you supposedly have more time.

Here are some ideas of how to scale back.

Create Lists List everything you require of yourself in a given day at home and the workplace. Look at the list, and remove a few items to be forwarded to the next day. In this way, rearrange self-expectations so they are spread out more broadly over the course of your week. You may already do this by writing a "to-do" list and then having to forward several items to the next day when you are unable to accomplish them. By choosing to spread out your expectations before you discover they won't fit into a given day, you see yourself as a success. When you continually deem yourself unable to meet daily goals, you will see yourself as one who regularly fails. This combination of unrealistic time demands and a perception of yourself as someone who is chronically behind schedule is a prescription for stress.

Double Your Travel Time If you know it takes you an average of twenty minutes to travel to work, give yourself forty minutes. You can reduce routine stress caused by traffic and other interferences that are out of your control.

Stop Squeezing Things into Your Schedule If you have to squeeze an appointment into an already full schedule, trade it for another commitment that is nonessential or can be done another day. If you cannot move something to another day, firmly set the boundary that you do not have time to squeeze in another commitment.

Schedule Inactive Time Our culture has become accomplishment oriented, devaluing time used for any experience that doesn't have tangible results. Activities such as relaxing on the grass with a child while gazing at clouds and daydreaming are deemed irrelevant. Schedule yourself time when you are not doing anything *productive*. Use this time for contemplation, play, listening, and so on.

8 ✱ Stop Overcommitting Yourself

Overcommitment brings on stress. Whenever you make commitments that exceed what you can actually do in a given day, week, month, or year, tensions mount. When your time is overcommitted, you will find you get behind, and your systems break down. Work put off until you have time for it becomes a bigger job than if you had planned enough time to do the work on a regular schedule. Relationships left untended because of overcommitment become strained. Then you need extra time to smooth over the hurt feelings that may arise when a relationship is neglected. In both work and personal relationships, overcommitment creates additional stress.

Here are some tips to keep you from overcommitting your time.

Never Say Yes Automatically Some people just can't seem to say no. They gain a reputation for being helpers and are put on everyone's volunteer list. If you have this tendency, deal with it. If you can't bring yourself to say no immediately, practice saying, "Let me check my calendar and get back to you." Then check to see if you can realistically say yes without creating more stress for yourself. If you genuinely want to help and have the time available, then call back and offer to help.

Keep a Calendar Make sure every commitment is in writing. If you keep a schedule only in your head, you will have to remember too much, and you may overestimate your time available. Be sure to write in time needed to prepare for and travel to and from each appointment.

Overestimate How Long Things Will Take
Give yourself up to double the amount of time you suppose you'll need for any given task or errand. Be sure to estimate time to travel and park and so on whenever you consider adding an appointment to your schedule.

Don't Pack Your Schedule Full of Productive Things You need some space and rest to keep
stress to a minimum. Plan some time for rest and refreshing in each day and week, then you won't have to deal with the stress of feeling like you are doing something wrong when you take time for activities that revive you.

Review Your Schedule with an Objective
Person Before beginning each week, review your commitments with someone who knows you and your lifestyle, perhaps a business associate, friend, or family member. Allow the other person to give you feedback from an objective point of view. If it seems you have overcommitted yourself, reschedule some things before the appointed time. In this way you can make sure you have time to fulfill your commitments and keep your nerves from being frazzled!

9 ✳ Seek Emotional Support

Studies show that getting emotional support during times of crisis reduces tension, depression, and fatigue and alleviates some physical symptoms of stress. Self-help emotional support groups such as Alcoholics Anonymous (AA) demonstrate that emotional support can help people learn to manage stress in healthy ways without resorting to the use of mood-altering drugs (e.g., alcohol).

When you avail yourself of emotional support, you learn that your reactions to stress are natural. When you reach out to others who care how you are feeling and perhaps share similar feelings and experiences, you discover new strength and a greater ability to cope.

Here are some ways to reach out and receive emotional support.

Reach Out to Friends Friends are a great source of emotional support if you invite them to be. In some times of crisis or tension, friends are not sure what to say or whether you would welcome their closeness. Ask your friends for their emotional support. Let them know that even though they may not be able to change your stressful circumstances, you welcome their emotional support. Tell them what you feel you need so they know where to start. If they do something you don't appreciate in an effort to support you, be gracious. Express appreciation for their care, and perhaps direct them to other ways of helping you that make you feel more comfortable.

Draw Close to Your Family
During times of stress, families tend either to draw together or to break apart. Be careful not to take your hostilities out on your family when stress overwhelms you. Instead, make a conscious effort to speak gently to one another; ask for a hug or other contact from your family that could give you emotional support.

See a Professional Counselor
If stress is so overpowering that your life is unmanageable, consider seeing a professional therapist. The person's expertise in helping people reduce inner tensions may benefit you. Regardless of the external crises you may face, a professional counselor may be able to point you to ways to cope that you are not currently practicing. A good counselor will also help you discover if physiological factors are contributing to your inability to handle the stress.

Join a Support Group
Support groups are centered on particular problems or issues. To locate a support group associated with your particular needs, contact local churches, medical centers, counseling offices, or government agencies. They should be able to direct you to a group to meet your needs. If you can't find a group, consider starting one of your own with others who are dealing with stressors similar to yours. You need not have a professional lead such a group. Just getting together

with others trying to meet the same challenges can give you strength and encouragement, whether you are undergoing treatment for cancer, raising preschool children as a single parent, or dealing with the effects of living with an addict.

Participate in a Self-Help Group There are many good self-help groups, and a substantial number are based on programs related to the Twelve-Step program devised by AA. When you consider a self-help group, first evaluate whether the principles upon which the program is founded agree with your personal values and beliefs. If you enter a group based on principles contrary to your values, you may find yourself feeling pressured to change your values rather than working on the issues you intended to work on. This kind of pressure creates additional stress.

Since self-help groups will be characterized by the personalities of the individuals in the group, don't give up looking for a group just because you didn't like one group. Keep looking until you find a group of people you feel you can relate to easily.

10 ✳ Manage Your Time

Each of us has twenty-four hours in a day. Planning to structure your time wisely can help you deal effectively with stress as it comes your way.

Create a Schedule for the Use of Your Time To keep your stress level manageable, you need a routine schedule for each day, even if you don't stick to it exactly. Having a structured schedule will keep you moving when you need to move and free you up to rest when you might otherwise push yourself to exhaustion.

- First, schedule the basics: sleeping, eating, grooming, exercising, and resting. Write out approximate times for each in a typical week.

- Next, schedule in your commitments that occur on a regular basis: work, classes, church, meetings, and so on.

- Schedule time to nurture the important relationships in your life: set aside time daily for each child, have a heart-to-heart chat with your spouse, and visit extended family and friends. These scheduled times for building relationships create opportunities to fulfill your role in the lives of those you love.

• Firmly schedule a day off each week when work demands are at a minimum. Relax, play, worship, and participate in nondemanding activities on this day off.

Block Out Interruptions Interruptions are always stressful. Careful planning can cut them to a minimum. When you are focused on a particular task within your schedule, take precautions to make sure you will experience as little interruption as possible. For example, use a telephone answering machine to screen calls that you will return later (during the time scheduled for returning calls). Post a "Do Not Disturb" sign. Attend to pressing needs before beginning your task so you won't be distracted in the middle of the task.

Take Control Over How You Spend Your Time Keep track of how you spend your time for one week. Then compare this time diary to how you would like to spend your time. Make decisions to use your time in keeping with your priorities and goals. If you are tied up in activities you resent, choose to revise your commitments to make the use of your time more meaningful to you.

Schedule More Time Than You Think You Will Need If you seem to always be running late or pressed for time, schedule your commitments farther apart.

Write Out a Daily Agenda By focusing your attention on the most essential things you seek to accomplish each day, you can more easily refocus your attention when something threatens your equilibrium. If you are going through uncertain times or a crisis, having a clear list of goals for today can keep you from despairing over possible difficulties ahead.

11 ✳ Find Healthy Ways to Vent Suppressed Anger

Suppressed anger can be a powerful source of internalized stress. There are healthy ways to get your anger out and relieve the building emotional pressure. Here are some ideas.

Tell God How Mad You Are If you are a person who sees anger as being bad, you may suppress your true feelings of anger. Perhaps you don't want to hurt anyone's feelings, or maybe you are afraid of the reaction you might get if you express your anger. If you are afraid to tell the target of your anger how you feel and why, try telling God.

Get away to a place where no one can hear you. Then address yourself to God and tell Him (out loud) precisely how you feel. Describe the incidents that prompted your anger, what you feel to be unjust, and so on. Even talk about your feelings of anger toward God. Many people suppress anger toward God because they believe that it is wrong to be angry with God. However, if you are angry with God, even if you believe you shouldn't be, you need to get rid of this suppressed anger.

Trust that God is big enough to handle your feelings. Express the anger you feel. Then if you believe there is something wrong with the real feelings you expressed, ask God's forgiveness. When you have exhausted your storehouse of anger, ask God to help you resolve any underlying issues and to find other healthy ways to rid yourself of suppressed anger.

Punch Something! Sometimes you can make yourself feel better by expressing anger physically. Be sure that whatever you choose to punch is not something (or someone) you might hurt. Punch out your anger in a pillow or punching bag. Chop firewood, pound nails, or hit baseballs in a batting cage. Anger creates real physical tension. Getting rid of the physical tension in physical ways can help you release the angry feelings at the same time.

Write a Letter Expressing Your Anger If
there are issues prompting your anger, express your outrage in words. If you are angry about something affecting your community, write a letter to the editor of your local paper. Say that you are angry; describe what prompts your anger and what you think should be done to make the situation right. The process of putting your anger into words is helpful—as is knowing that you have taken action to use your anger constructively.

Take Responsibility for Your Feelings
Counselors and health-care professionals agree that having a greater sense of control over life reduces stress. If you believe others have the power to control your emotions, you give up control over your response. Using "I" statements, such as "I am angry," reflects taking responsi-

bility for your anger rather than blaming others for how you feel. Others really don't have the power to "make you mad," even if they wrong you in some way. By accepting responsibility for your feelings, you gain a sense of control over your life and reduce stress.

12 ✳ Get a Pet

Anyone who has known the love of a faithful pet can easily
understand that having the right pet can reduce stress.
Studies have confirmed that when people pet an animal,
there are calming effects that can be measured. Their
blood pressure and heart rates go down. Cardiac patients
who have pets are shown to live longer than those who do
not. Pets can make you laugh. They give and receive love
without ever having an argument with you. The compan-
ionship of a pet can alleviate loneliness and give you
something to care for. Besides, a pet is always glad to see
you and appreciates your company without requiring you
to perform.

Here are some ideas of various pets and how they
might reduce your stress.

Fish Watching the graceful movements of fish and
other underwater life can calm those who are upset.
Aquariums are sometimes used in elegant restaurants to
set a tranquil mood, in children's waiting rooms of doctors' offices to distract from fear, and in counseling offices
to promote a nonthreatening atmosphere.

Some doctors and therapists recommend that people in
high-stress jobs set up an aquarium in the office. Consider

getting an aquarium filled with colorful tropical fish for someplace you encounter stress.

Cats and Kittens Who can resist a playful kitten? A kitten has no regard for the importance of the report you are working on or whether you have a final exam tomorrow morning. A kitten lives for the joy of the moment. A kitten can often entice you to put the pressures aside for a moment of spontaneous fun. If you don't want to get a kitten of your own, try visiting a pet store and just playing with the kittens.

A cat can offer a calming effect just by being near you in its gentle easy way. The fluffy warmth of a cat nestled in your lap or at your feet invites a moment of relaxation. Its gentle purr is much more soothing than the tick of the clock. Besides all of this, cats are highly independent and require little daily care.

Dogs and Puppies Puppies insist on having fun. Some dogs provide hours of relaxation as they play with you—fetching a ball, tugging on a rope, or catching Frisbees on the beach. Not only do you get the emotional benefits of having a pet, a dog can remind you to take regular breaks for exercise. Having a dog who requires a walk at regular intervals can excuse you from other stressful duties.

13 ✳ Reduce Your Debts

One of the most common sources of stress is financial worries. When you are in the habit of living in debt, you invite stress. Being able to accommodate unforeseen financial changes reduces the level of stress you will face. If you are debt-free and the economy takes a dip or you lose your job, the effects are mild compared to the possible consequences for someone in debt. If your family is in debt, any financial setback may herald significant losses of things you rely on. The family living debt-free is never faced with the fear of this kind of loss or the loss of reputation associated with a poor credit rating.

Marriage counselors note that financial problems weigh heavily in marital difficulties. If you and your spouse have a habit of overspending or argue regularly about money issues, these marital problems can be eased by working together to devise a financial plan in which you learn to live within your means.

Here are some ideas to help you reduce your debts.

Seek Advice Read books that teach you how to change your financial habits and how to convert to a debt-free way of life.

Take a class in financial management and apply what you learn.

Consult a financial or credit counselor.

Identify Goals   Set a goal to eliminate one debt by a specific time. Once that debt is gone, add the amount you were paying on that debt to the regular amount you pay on another debt.

Make your progress visible by creating charts depicting your steps toward paying off your debts.

Plan Payments   Use any unexpected income (such as a raise or bonus) toward debt reduction. Apply even small amounts toward a specific debt.

Use savings to pay off debts. You will save the higher rate in interest (you've been paying on credit). Just keep enough in savings to act as a buffer. If you have to, you can always get a cash advance, but in the meantime you're saving money on interest.

Arrange for direct payment to creditors from your paycheck or checking account.

Transfer debt to lower-interest credit cards, and put the interest saved toward debt reduction. Consolidate debts on a lower-interest loan.

Maximize Payments   Refinance to reduce interest on your home mortgage or other considerable loans.

Pay off your mortgage on a slightly faster schedule (biweekly instead of monthly, fifty dollars extra each month, or one extra payment toward the principal each year). You can save tens of thousands of dollars over the life of your mortgage.

Delay Purchases   Put off buying a new car for a year longer than usual. Do necessary maintenance and repairs. Use the difference between repair costs and the previous car payment toward debt reduction.

14 ✳ Express Your Feelings with Words

William Shakespeare wrote in *Macbeth,* "Give sorrow words: the grief that does not speak, whispers in the over wrought heart and bids it break."

Communication with another human being is one of the best stress reducers known. Words help you escape feelings of loneliness and despair. Knowing that someone cares and is trying to understand what you are experiencing can give you the strength to go on, despite any adversity.

Isolation in disheartening circumstances increases the weight of tensions. That is why being put in solitary confinement is such a stressful condition. Prisoners of war throughout history have created elaborate communication codes because being connected to others makes stress in times of crisis manageable. Emotional isolation also increases stress. The feeling that you are suffering alone, that no one understands, that you dare not confide in anyone, makes stressful situations weigh on you more heavily.

Here are some ways to express your feelings.

Put Your Feelings into Words Use some means of creative expression to formulate your feelings into words. You may want to record in a journal what happened and what it meant to you. You may want to describe the feelings, the sense of loss, your source of hope and strength. Write poetry, songs, stories, and so on to give your problems and grief understandable form. Write letters to people with whom you want to communicate. You may not choose to send the letters, but the process of getting out what you are thinking and feeling can relieve pent-up or confused thoughts and emotions.

Share Your Writings with Someone Once you have clearly expressed your feelings, problems, or grief in words, find someone who would appreciate seeing what you have expressed.

Talk to a Good Listener When someone listens to you, the care and attentiveness validate your feelings and concerns. When someone listens, you know you are not alone.

Confer with Someone Going Through Similar Stressful Circumstances If your primary source of stress is from an identifiable stressor, talk to others who are going through or have gone through similar stressful conditions.

15 ✳ Create a Calming Home Environment

When you establish a home, you have the potential to create a place where you escape the stresses of the outside world. Here are some ideas for making your home less stress inducing, perhaps even calming.

Plan for Order Make sure the design of your home accommodates activities important to the development of each family member. For example, if you have small children, babyproof by keeping electrical outlets covered and poisons out of reach. You reduce the stress of continually worrying about safety. If you have school students, provide a place for them to study with adequate lighting and necessary supplies. You reduce the stress of having to constantly respond to unmet needs by looking for pens or trying to find a dictionary during study times.

If you have family members with differing tastes in entertainment, create separate rooms that allow each to enjoy a preference occasionally. Instead of having to decide to play Nintendo, watch football, or read quietly, set up a Nintendo monitor in one room, television in another, and a reading lamp in a quiet part of the house.

Create a Refuge from the World Don't just let the clamor of the world come barging in. You can choose to screen your calls, unplug your phone, turn off the television, or do numerous other things that give you a rest from the world's hue and cry.

Guard Nourishing Moments at Home

Family meals can be times of relaxation and enjoyment, but you have to plan for that to happen. Let all family members know when they are expected for meals. If both spouses work outside the home, share the work entailed in creating family meals. Celebrate your meals with fresh flowers and music.

Read bedtime stories to children or to your spouse. Reading stories is a great way to share special moments and relax before bed. All children love stories, particularly when read aloud by a loving parent. Even adults enjoy hearing a story read aloud (consider the market for books on audiotape).

Keep Work Limited to One Specific Place

If you can, keep your work and home separate. If your office is in your home or if you must bring work home, keep work supplies limited to one place or room. When you are not working, close the door to that room.

Establish Family Routines Routines give a sense of order and help us have a feeling of normalcy. Try to maintain regular routines for eating, sleeping, bathing, dressing, and doing other daily functions.

Hold Regular Family Meetings   Use these scheduled times to make decisions, solve problems, plan for the future, coordinate schedules, share information, and keep in touch with the significant events and emotions in the lives of family members.

16 ✳ Go Fishing

Fishing has long been enjoyed as a way to relax. In this goal-oriented world, there seem to be few acceptable excuses for sitting around doing nothing. Fishing gives you the excuse you need. When you go fishing, you are focused on a goal (catching a fish) that requires you to remain still, get outdoors in the beauty of nature, and wait quietly.

Take a Break If it's been a while since you've wet a hook, consider taking a fishing trip. You can sit on a dock over a quiet lake, stand on a pier above the ocean, take a rowboat out away from shore, wade knee-deep in a rushing river, spend a weekend on a commercial fishing barge, cut a hole in the ice, or take a week off to fish in the wilderness. Any way you choose, fishing is practically guaranteed to reduce stress. Just try not to take your cellular phone along for the trip!

Here's all you have to do.

Gear Up Locate or buy fishing gear (some establishments near lakes even rent fishing gear for the afternoon).

Decide where fishing is available in your area or where you want to go to find a fishing spot.

Check with the fish and wildlife service to get the necessary fishing license.

Choose a companion (or more than one). Or if you prefer, go alone.

Just Go   Plan the time off.

Put out a sign that reads "Gone Fishing" and go.

17 ✳ Get a Massage

Massage is an effective way to deal with the physical symptoms of stress. Here are some tips to remember when getting a massage.

For a Relaxing Massage If you are seeking stress relief from your massage, it is something you don't want to rush. A full body massage should take approximately one hour.

Here is what you should expect from a massage. Since clothes are restrictive, you will be asked to disrobe, and you will be draped with a sheet. You will lie on a massage table. A trained massage therapist will be careful to respect your modesty and will never touch breasts or genitals. You will probably feel more comfortable with a same-sex therapist.

Dim lighting and soothing music often help you relax while receiving a massage.

For a Certified Massage The American Massage Therapy Association certifies massage therapists. Ask to see the credentials of anyone claiming to be a certified massage therapist.

Be sure the massage therapist is aware of any physical

pain you are experiencing or of previous injuries. The therapist should interview you preceding your first visit to gain this information. If not, speak up. Also remember that there are differing schools of massage. Some techniques are quite gentle while others incorporate deep massage that can be mildly painful if the therapist is massaging tensed muscles. Anytime you are experiencing pain, tell the therapist, and ask the person to adjust to your needs and preference.

You can find a certified massage therapist in your area by getting a referral from a local doctor of chiropractic or contacting the American Massage Therapy Association by writing 1329 West Pratt Boulevard, Chicago, Illinois 60626 or calling 312-761-2682. Many chiropractic offices have certified massage therapists available in the office. Many massage therapists advertise in the yellow pages of the telephone directory. Their ads will usually note "nonsexual massage" to distinguish their services from those of less-reputable establishments.

Some community colleges offer courses in massage for couples. Check with your local college regarding these classes.

For a Self-Massage   You can relax tension pent up in muscles by massaging, rubbing, or gently drumming the area of tension with your fists.

To stimulate blood flow to your scalp and relieve tension, take a handful of hair in each hand and gently tug for a few seconds, then relax your grip.

Tension headaches (which are caused by muscular contractions in the head and neck) can be eased by massaging your temples, scalp, neck, and forehead. Before beginning your face and head massage, wrap your forehead or back of the neck with a hot or cold damp towel. That will relax the muscles before you begin your massage. Use your fingers to gently massage areas around and under your eyes, back of the neck, and scalp.

18 ✹ Treat Your Feet

Your feet routinely take enormous amounts of stress and do so very well. Treating your feet tenderly can dramatically relax you and reduce muscle tension. Here are some ideas for treating your feet to reduce stress.

Wear Proper Shoes Wear appropriate shoes for the activity you undertake. If you are on your feet much of the day, avoid extremely high heels, and make sure your feet have adequate support. A wide variety of shoes and footwear on the market meets the particular needs of any occupation or athletic activity. Consult your podiatrist or local athletic footwear outlet for a recommendation of what would be best for you.

Always make sure you have the proper fit in footwear. A poor fit can cause chafing and blisters and create muscle spasms in the foot.

Massage Feet A good foot massage can relieve soreness, promote blood circulation, reduce foot swelling, and hasten healing of foot injuries. Here are some tips for a great at-home foot massage:

- Soak feet in warm to hot water, using a foot bath solution that you can purchase at a pharmacy or in the health and beauty section of a supermarket. You may want to get a foot massage device that holds water, keeps the water warm, and vibrates your feet while you relax. It is a wonderful addition to the daily routine of anyone who spends much time standing or walking.

- Have a partner towel dry each foot and follow this procedure: gently stroke the muscles on the bottom of the foot, kneading muscles in a circular motion with the thumb. Stretch the foot, point the toes, flex the foot, and massage the Achilles tendon at the back of the ankle. Pull gently on each toe, and rotate in a circular motion several times.

- Massage feet and calves with foot cream or body lotion.

- Prop your feet up and rest for at least twenty minutes.

Get a Pedicure   Most beauty or nail salons provide pedicures. A thorough pedicure will include foot and calf massage, which can help you relax.

See a Doctor   If you have recurrent pain in your feet, see a podiatrist.

19 ✳ Use Commuting Time to Unwind

Commuting to and from work or school can become a recurrent source of stress, particularly if you must battle traffic to do so. Here are some ideas for making the commute less stressful.

Adjust Time Schedule more than enough time to get to and from your destination.

If driving in traffic creates stress for you, consider the possibility of adjusting your work hours so that you commute at a time when traffic is not at its height.

Learn Something Use commuting time to learn something new. Many excellent training and educational programs are on audiotape. If you drive and have a cassette tape deck, use your commuting time to learn a foreign language, expand your vocabulary, motivate greater achievement, increase your business knowledge, become a better parent, improve management ability, or study any number of other subjects. These audio teaching programs are available at bookstores, through television advertisements, at libraries, and through mail-order catalogs. You can also get best-selling nonfiction books on audio.

Listen to Music   Keep a selection of music tapes in your car. Choose music you enjoy. Include a few tapes of music you know will have a calming effect on you.

Escape   Use commuting time to listen to the latest best-selling fiction books on audiotape. Listening to fiction is a great escape. If you have a hard time changing gears to get out of a working mode, focusing your attention on a story can take your mind off work while your body heads home.

Let Someone Else Drive   If driving is stressful for you, consider using public transportation or carpooling. If you take public transportation, use the free time to focus on something other than work. Perhaps read a novel, practice a relaxing hobby like knitting or crocheting, or solve crossword puzzles.

20 ✳ Have a Warm Relaxing Drink

You can enjoy many warm drinks that will relax you rather than pep you up. Since caffeine and alcohol act as artificial stimulants and depressants, limit or avoid drinks with either substance. Alcohol in particular promises short-lived stress relief.

Consider these soothing drinks that pose no health risk.

Herbal Teas The wide variety of herbal teas on the market offers such a range of flavors that you are sure to find one you enjoy. You can purchase herbal teas in most supermarkets and health food stores. Herbal teas are all-natural blends of herbs, spices, and fruit flavors. Some of the most popular flavors are peppermint (which kids love if served with a candy cane to stir it), chamomile, apple-cinnamon, orange-spice, lemon, and blackberry. You may want to purchase a sampler pack initially until you find a flavor you enjoy.

Warm Milk Warm milk before bedtime has long been thought to induce sleep and hasten relaxation. One reason is that warming the milk releases the amino acid tryptophan, which acts as a natural mild tranquilizer. You can warm milk in a saucepan on the stove, in a double boiler, or in the microwave. You may want to add a few drops of vanilla for sweetening and a wonderful aroma.

Hot Chocolate Milk
Hot chocolate is a winter-time favorite. You can heat milk and cocoa powder or syrup on the stove, or you may prefer a prepackaged powder ready for you to add hot water, stir, and enjoy. There are varieties sweetened with sugar substitutes, single serving packets you can take with you, and even some with prepackaged mini-marshmallows.

For a Christmas treat, top hot chocolate with whipped cream and red-and-green sugar sprinkles, and stir with a candy cane. The candy cane melts to make a great mint chocolate flavor.

Chocolate does contain caffeine. Take care to drink it in moderation.

Hot Apple Cider
Warm up apple juice or cider, and stir with cinnamon sticks. You may also enjoy the flavor of tying whole cloves and cinnamon in cheesecloth or a tea ball and allowing the apple cider to simmer until the spices flavor the cider.

21 ✳ Play Video Games

Many people are recognizing the therapeutic effect of playing video games. Although this pastime seems to be most popular with young people, many adults are discovering that taking a turn at the controls helps them unwind. Perhaps you have noticed how utterly absorbed players appear while playing the games. Some parents complain that their children seem almost hypnotized, unable to be distracted by anything around them. This mesmerizing effect may be just what you are looking for to remove you from the stresses you would like to keep from distracting you! Why not give it a try?

There are many varieties of video games. There are word games, such as Wheel of Fortune, Hangman, and Scrabble. There are combat games; opposing characters battle against one another. There are obstacle games; the characters must overcome progressively difficult obstacles to achieve a goal.

Here are some tips about the types of video games and how to get started playing.

Game Systems for the Home Computer game systems include Nintendo, Super Nintendo, and Sega Genesis. Each system uses games designed specifically for that system, which are not interchangeable. You can rent game systems and games from many video rental stores and bring them home to hook up to a standard television monitor. You can also purchase game systems for home use (or wait until your child is at school and use the system). Most kids who are proficient at playing video games enjoy showing off their skills for parents and teaching basic skills to newcomers.

Video Arcades Video arcades are found at most shopping malls and family fun centers. Miniarcades are in pizza parlors, movie theaters, and other places young people congregate. Play typically costs between a quarter and fifty cents per game.

Computer Software Stores Most computer software stores have a section of games. Some have a game system set up so that prospective buyers can try their skill. The sales representatives at such stores should be able to explain various games to you and help you get started in playing with or purchasing a game system.

Hand-Held Video Games Many small video games similar to the games played on a computer monitor are highly portable and can be tucked away in purse, briefcase, or pocket as a readily available stress-reducing tool.

Interactive Compact Disc Video Games

Interactive compact disc units for use with your television are comparatively expensive (costing about eight times as much as a basic video game system), but the scope and educational value of these games are superior.

22 ✳ Immerse Yourself in a Spa

You can choose from many kinds of spas. All of them are designed to help you relax and reduce stress. Just because you may not own a Jacuzzi does not mean the benefits of a spa are out of reach. Consider these options.

A Health Club   You can combine the stress-reducing effects of getting physical exercise with relaxing in the spa or pool by joining a health club. One of the advantages to this option is that you don't have to incorporate the responsibility of maintaining a spa into your schedule.

Bathtub Whirlpool Insert   Some products insert into your standard bathtub and create a bubbling whirlpool action. In this way you can turn any bath into a stress-reducing bubble bath.

Massaging Shower Head   These shower heads use water pressure and pulse action to turn your shower into a relaxing massage. They are easily fitted onto any standard shower and are available at most department stores or home improvement stores.

Home Spa or Hot Tub An outdoor freestanding
spa or hot tub provides a place to unwind both physically
and mentally. Spa dealerships sell spas and hot tubs in a
wide range of sizes, shapes, and prices.

Jacuzzi Bathtub If you are in the process of re-
modeling or building your home, you might consider in-
stalling a bathtub that doubles as a spa. These tubs are
larger than a standard tub and have water jets built in. You
can use the tub with or without the water jets turned on.

23 ✳ Make Yourself Laugh

Laughter is a pleasant way to rid yourself of tension. You have probably heard that laughter is the best medicine. This saying is based in fact. Medical research has shown that laughter actually has therapeutic effects within the body. Laughing speeds up your heart rate, releases endorphins into your system (which act as a natural pain reliever), and helps relieve stress. Do yourself a favor. Give yourself a healthy dose of laughter.

In the midst of a difficult time of life there is always room for a little laughter. Laughter can lighten the seemingly overwhelming tension so that you can deal with difficulties in manageable doses. You can make choices that bring laughter into your life, even during stressful circumstances. You can make a conscious effort to look for what is humorous and to expose yourself to things that are funny. Even if the laughter is only for a moment, it can be tremendously refreshing.

Here are some ideas of ways to make yourself laugh.

Think of Things That Make You Laugh
Think about funny moments, the antics of small children, times when you laughed hard, embarrassing moments, and so on.

Do Something Fun or Funny   Choose an activity that you consider fun—something like going to an amusement park or waterskiing. Go out and do it.

Rent a Comedy Video   The comedy section of your local video store offers many options to make you laugh. *Bill Cosby Himself* is especially enjoyable if you have small children; the sketch he does on parenting is hysterical.

Watch Classic Comedy Reruns   Footage of "I Love Lucy," Abbott and Costello, Charlie Chaplin, or other classic comedians is hard to resist. *Reader's Digest Video* has a three-volume set of the best laughs of all time. Or check your television listings for reruns.

Read a Funny Book   Get a book from the comedy or humor section of your local bookstore, and read it out loud to someone. Laughing together can reduce stress in a relationship like nothing else. Many book-length collections of popular comic strips are almost irresistibly funny.

Tickle a Loved One   Chances are good that you may get tickled, too.

Try Not to Laugh   Laughing is one of those things that people seem to do when trying not to. Announce that there is to be no laughter for thirty minutes. For some reason, the whole world takes on comic appeal when we tell ourselves not to laugh. To heighten the stakes, make a game of it. Invite a friend or child to try to make you laugh while you try not to laugh.

24 ✳ Meditate on Things That Do Not Change

Stress is always associated with changes that affect us. When you perceive changes as threatening, your level of stress increases. Life is constantly changing in ways that are, for the most part, out of your complete control. Anything you can do to increase your sense of security in the face of uncertainty will help you cope with the normal stresses of life. Thinking about the things that are unchanging helps you cope with the things that do change. Here are some things to think about.

The Unchanging Nature of God The Bible says that God does not change. He is reliable and predictable, solid as a rock amidst the shifting sands of life. Meditating on God's nature can increase your sense of ultimate security. A strong belief in a loving and unchanging God gives you something firm upon which to rely during uncertain times. Knowing who holds your future can ease your concerns about what the future may hold. During uncertain times, remember these quotes from the Bible regarding the unchanging nature of God:

"For the mountains shall depart
And the hills be removed,

But My kindness shall not
   depart from you,
Nor shall My covenant of peace be removed,"
Says the Lord, who has mercy
   on you (Isa. 54:10).

"For I am the Lord, I do not change;
Therefore you are not
   consumed, O sons of Jacob.
Yet from the days of your fathers
You have gone away from My ordinances
And have not kept them.
Return to Me, and I will return to you,"
Says the Lord of hosts (Mal. 3:6–7).

Through the Lord's mercies we
   are not consumed,
Because His compassions fail not.
They are new every morning;
Great is Your faithfulness.
"The Lord is my portion," says my soul,
"Therefore I hope in Him!" (Lam. 3:22–24).

Jesus Christ is the same yesterday, today, and forever
(Heb. 13:8).

The Unchanging Aspects of Nature

Regardless of the stresses and changes you are going through, life goes on. The earth goes on spinning, revolving around the sun. The sun rises and sets. The waves crash

on the seashore. The seasons follow one another in se-
quence: spring, summer, autumn, and winter. Birds mi-
grate. Salmon still swim upstream at their appointed time.
Focusing on what remains the same may help you get
through life's changes.

25 ✳ Reduce Role Overload at Home

Home used to be seen as a place of refuge from a stressful world, a place where comforting routines made life more calm and secure. The image of a family gathered around the dinner table, having a leisurely discussion after enjoying a home-cooked meal, is no longer the norm. A more up-to-date image of modern home life might be something like this: Mom and Dad arrive home after leaving work and picking up the children from school or day care. They drove through a fast-food restaurant to grab dinner on the way. Following a hurried dinner, which may be eaten in front of the television, various activities vie for attention.

One result of rapidly changing role definitions within our culture is extra stress at home. In addition to trying to create quality family experiences in a limited amount of time, tasks that make a home run smoothly are piling up. Whenever the unexpected happens, such as an illness, the stress on the family may rise to excessive levels.

Changing roles also affect expectations within the family, and changing expectations often create conflict. A woman who got married expecting her husband to provide financially for the family (as was the norm a generation ago) may have to work out of economic necessity. A husband who grew up expecting his wife to focus her energies solely on managing their home may have to adjust to the reality that his wife chooses to pursue a career or must work to meet the family budget. A single parent who never expected to be raising children alone may have to handle all parental and home management responsibilities.

These kinds of role changes require renegotiating family relationships on an ongoing basis and dealing with your emotional reaction to life that may be quite different from what you imagined for yourself. These changes mean that everyone must adjust expectations and skills to meet the challenges of multiple roles. These changes also mean that there is often a great deal of stress associated with being at home.

Here are some ideas to help you cope with role overload at home.

Clarify Expectations with All Family Members Discuss and decide who will be responsible for specific tasks that make home life run smoothly. Be careful to weigh the responsibilities according to each individual's age and ability. Once these expectations are clarified, write out job descriptions, and have family members accept responsibility for the role they play in making home life workable.

Be Aware and Sensitive Be aware of and sensitive to the other role demands on each family member. Hold family meetings on a weekly basis so everyone can learn about what is happening with others in the family. The roles of student, employee, employer, supervisor, friend, team player, club member, and so on come with demands.

Help One Another Manage Outside Pressures

Discuss the pressures on each family member from outside the home. Then be sensitive to these pressures as they come and go. If a child has a major school project due, help the child budget time wisely, and perhaps ask others to pitch in to relieve some pressure of home duties the week it is due. If a parent or spouse has pressing demands at work or school, lighten the load at home temporarily.

Lower Standards on Low-Priority Items

If you or other family members are experiencing role overload, there is no way your home can run as beautifully as if someone devoted full-time effort to home management. Therefore, don't demand perfection. Instead, prioritize what matters most to your family, and lower your standards regarding things that do not matter as much.

Eliminate Overwhelming Roles

If you are feeling overcome by the demands being placed on you, try this: list every role you play and every title you hold (e.g., parent, employee, troop leader, club member, employer, committee head, volunteer, and so on). Then put them in order of importance and list how much time each role demands weekly. Decide which ones you can live without, and excuse yourself from playing those roles.

For roles you cannot excuse yourself from (e.g., parent or employee if you must work), consider how you could change your way of fulfilling this role to relieve stress. For example, if you must work but your job is too stressful, get a different job that you are better able to manage. If parenting is putting a strain on you, join a parents support group or take parenting classes to improve your parenting skills.

26 ＊ Stretch at Your Desk

The National Institute for Occupational Safety and Health identifies managers, secretaries, and administrators as having high rates of stress-related illnesses. These are typically desk jobs that involve focused concentration, anxiety, and mental stress. Mental stress can take its toll on your body in the form of muscle tension and headaches. Taking a brief time to stretch at your desk can divert your attention from anxiety-producing work and relieve the physical symptoms of stress that lead to physical problems.

Stretching Routines Here are some tips for stretching at your desk:

- Always stretch slowly and leisurely. Imagine yourself stretching like a cat; use deliberate movements.

- Start your stretching routine with a few slow, deep breaths.

- Reach your arms in front of you, and spread your fingers as far apart as you can. Then slowly curl your fingers into a fist, and stretch out again as wide as possible. Follow this by touching each finger to your thumb and wiggling all your fingers.

- Lift your arms high above your head while yawning or opening your jaw as wide as you can.

- Lace your fingers behind your neck, and slowly bring your chin to your chest, stretching your neck muscles. Bring your head back up while keeping fingers laced behind your neck, and slowly rotate your upper torso to the right, then left.

- Stand and reach your arms above your head as far as you can, then gently reach down to touch your shoulders, knees, and toes. If you cannot stand, perform the same stretches while seated, but when reaching for your toes, bring your head onto your knees, and allow your arms to dangle toward the floor.

- Holding onto the sides of your chair, place one foot flat on the floor, and extend the other leg in front of you. Alternate pointing your toes and flexing the foot several times. Trade leg positions and repeat.

- Hold your arms behind you and interlace your fingers. Then raise your arms as far as you can to stretch your back, chest, shoulders, and upper arms.

27 ✳ Choose Soothing Colors

Studies show that colors have a demonstrable effect on levels of stress. The book *Managing Stress from Morning to Night* reports the following:

- The body is less stimulated by black than other colors.

- Blue may elevate mood.

- Brown may be calming.

- Green may actually increase stress.

- Pink may have a tranquilizing effect.

- Red is an arousing, stimulating color.

- Yellow may reduce boredom.

These conclusions are drawn from scientific studies examining the body's response to various colors by measuring mood reaction, blood pressure, oxygen levels, electrical conductivity of the skin, risk-taking behavior, levels of aggression, and hostility.

You probably haven't been part of a scientific study of the effects of color on stress levels, but if you think about it, you can probably see an association between color and stress from personal experience. The tranquility of a baby's nursery decorated in pale shades of pink. The reaction you have had when someone arrives for an interview dressed in red. The calming effect of a doctor's reception room decorated in earth tones and warm browns. These connections between color and stress are fairly obvious.

Marsha Rae is a prominent interior designer who teaches classes on how to choose colors to create a particular effect. She notes that people under stress are drawn to the color purple. She also predicts that purple will be the color of the nineties. Is it any wonder? She suggests that whenever you find yourself attracted to purple, you should check your stress level.

If color does affect mood and stress level, as scientific studies and personal experience indicate, you can reduce stress by controlling some of the colors in your surroundings. Here are some suggestions.

Your Workplace

Decorate your work space in colors that calm or uplift you. If you cannot paint your surroundings, you can bring in color by using fabric, silk flowers, artwork, and other colorful objects that are easily removed.

Your Home

Paint each room of your home to coincide with its function(s). Choose calming shades for the bedroom or rooms used for retreat from stress. Try blue in areas where studying takes place. Use uplifting yellow and white in the kitchen or breakfast nook. If you don't feel confident to make these major decorating decisions on your own, consult an interior designer who can help you select colors to meet the needs of your family in the home.

Your Clothes   Color coordinate your wardrobe to affect your mood and present the impression you desire to make. Color consultants can help you choose colors in wardrobe and cosmetics that match your natural coloring. When you look great, you will feel better about yourself all around.

28 ✳ Tell Someone Your Secrets

Keeping secrets can be very stressful. A recent news report exemplifies this fact. A well-respected doctor, in his early fifties, seemed to be in good health but died suddenly of a heart attack. Upon his death, he left behind three widows—he had been married to them simultaneously. None of the three had known of the other two. The busy doctor hid his secret life behind the smoke screen of a hectic hospital schedule. The truth is that he was busy covering his tracks. Can you imagine the level of stress the man lived with every moment of every day? Is it any wonder that he died from a stress-induced illness?

This example is extreme. However, if you are keeping secrets, an accompanying level of stress is involved: the stress of struggling with your conscience, the stress of worrying over what may happen if you are found out, and the stress of having to cover up what you are trying to hide.

Telling someone your secrets can profoundly reduce your stress level if it is done in a safe environment. But if your secrets are exposed to someone who may react against you, telling your secrets could be more stressful than keeping them. Therefore, carefully choose when, how, and to whom to reveal your secrets. Here are some guidelines to keep in mind.

Start by Being Honest with Yourself If you are dealing with something shameful or related to addictive-compulsive behavior, look for a Twelve-Step group associated with your condition. One of the tenets of these groups is to become honest with yourself, God, and another human being. These groups are committed to keeping shared secrets confidential while offering support from others who have experienced similar struggles.

Minimize Risks You must take the utmost care to find someone who is safe to tell your secrets. If you keep secrets about yourself out of fear of rejection, don't risk rejection when first opening up. Instead, share your secrets with someone who is legally or morally bound to keep your confidence. Seek out a licensed therapist, who is bound by law to keep your confidence, or a member of the clergy who adheres to confidentiality as a strict practice of his or her moral code.

Here are some qualities to look for in a confidant:

- Humility

- Acceptance of others

- Compassion

- Nonjudgmental attitude

- A good listening ear

- Faithfulness in keeping confidences

- No vested interest—nothing to lose or gain by what you reveal

- Optimistic approach to life

Tell Your Spouse?   You may be inclined to confide in your spouse but wonder if that is a good choice. Ideally, you should be able to confide in and trust your spouse to love you for better or for worse. Since we don't live in an ideal world, carefully consider at what point and pace to reveal your secrets to your spouse. You may require the assistance of a qualified marriage counselor.

29 ✻ Practice Good Posture

Poor posture can lead to muscular tension, headaches, dizziness, damage to joints, and other physical stress-related symptoms. Deep breathing, which reduces stress, is impaired by poor posture. Improving your posture when sitting and standing allows for greater flow of oxygen, spinal alignment, and better overall health. You can reduce physical stress by learning to eliminate poor posture and replace it with good posture.

Consider these examples of poor posture:

- Slumping in your chair

- Hunching your shoulders

- Curving your back

- Drooping your head

- Shuffling your feet when walking

- Tilting your pelvis

- Tilting your head and neck to one side

Here is a good posture checklist to evaluate yourself.

When Sitting Keep your feet flat on the floor in front of your chair. Make sure the chair height is appropriate to allow you to do this while keeping your legs bent at a forty-five-degree angle. If your knees are propped up higher than your hips or if you must stretch your toes to reach the floor, your chair is the wrong size for you.

Keep your head erect. Avoid allowing your neck to tilt forward. Imagine a string attached to the center of the top of your head, lifting gently up until your head and neck are aligned with your spine.

When Working at a Computer If you use a computer monitor, determine whether it is adjusted to the proper height. Sit in your chair with your hands placed on your keyboard. Close your eyes and assume a position with your back straight and head comfortably erect, facing the direction of the screen. When you open your eyes, you should be looking directly at the screen without having to raise or lower your gaze. Instead of adjusting your posture to the computer monitor, move the height of the monitor to meet your gaze.

When Writing or Typing A straight-backed chair is best if you are working at a desk where you are writing. If you spend much time typing, be sure your chair gives you adequate back support.

When Standing or Walking Keep your head centered over your trunk and erect, shoulders back, chest up, pelvis straight, and feet forward.

Don't hold yourself in a stiff military pose. Instead, check to make sure your body is aligned as it should be while keeping your muscles relaxed. Your alignment should be such that from the back, your spine is straight with your head directly above the spine. From the side view, your spine will form a slight curve somewhat like an *S*.

You may want to see a chiropractor to help you with the effects of poor posture over a long period of time.

30 ✷ Eat a Healthy Diet

A healthy diet is a basic foundation for a healthy life, including being able to manage stress well. When you are under stress, your body demands more nutrients than it ordinarily would. Also, being under stress may trigger an eating cycle that actually makes you less able to handle stress. You may stop eating to focus on whatever is causing stress, or you may compulsively eat comfort foods (usually high in fat and sugar) to make yourself feel better. Either way, your body has an added stress of an unbalanced diet at a time when it needs a supply of nutritious food.

Stress is also known to deplete the body of B vitamins and vitamin C. B vitamins are part of the process producing biochemicals in your brain cells to pass messages from one nerve ending to the next. When you are deficient in B vitamins, you may experience mental fatigue, confusion, depression, and other symptoms that make you less able to cope with stress.

An adequate supply of vitamin C is necessary for your body to recover from physical stresses such as pregnancy, surgery, burns, broken bones, or certain kinds of drug therapy. Studies also indicate that vitamin C supplements can prevent some adverse effects of common industrial pollutants, helping your body cope with the physical effects of some chemical hazards in the environment.

Each individual has a unique capacity for mentally being able to handle stress. However, everyone can handle stress better when the diet is rich in B vitamins and vitamin C.

Here are some ideas to help you eat a healthy diet, which will help you manage stress.

B Vitamins   Eat foods naturally rich in B vitamins, such as beef, chicken, eggs, liver, milk, dairy foods, pork, brewer's yeast, dark green leafy vegetables, whole grains, enriched breads and cereals, nuts, seeds, and wheat germ.

Natural Sources of Vitamin C   Your body needs thirty to sixty milligrams of vitamin C daily. You can get vitamin C from fresh fruits and vegetables, especially citrus fruits, tomatoes, potatoes, dark green vegetables, and green peppers.

Supplements   Although some experts advise getting your vitamins and minerals in whole foods whenever possible, you can take a daily multivitamin-mineral supplement that supplies daily requirements, or supplement your diet with B vitamins and vitamin C. These sometimes come in packets called stress tabs.

Frozen Foods   If you are too busy or too stressed to cook balanced meals for yourself, choose frozen meals that are geared to healthy, balanced diets. Several brands, such as Weight Watchers, Healthy Choice, Jenny Craig, and so on, cater to health-conscious consumers.

Snacks   Keep healthy snacks on hand to sustain your energy and help you resist those high-fat and high-sugar snacks you may gravitate toward when you are under stress. Try keeping fresh vegetables and fruits, whole grain crackers, and low-fat yogurt readily available.

Caffeine   Wean yourself from caffeine and other stimulants. When you feel the need to perk yourself up, reach for snacks high in protein rather than caffeine—hard-boiled eggs, nuts, seeds, milk, cheese, or peanut butter. Caffeine eventually will make you jittery and may compound your stress. Because caffeine can be addictive, be cautious when weaning yourself away from it. If you cut yourself off abruptly, you may experience painful symptoms of withdrawal, such as severe headaches. Gradually decrease your caffeine intake over the course of several days or even a few weeks.

31 ✳ Pray

Prayer can help you manage stress in many ways. The very act of stopping what you are doing to pray will give you a moment of relief. If you bow your head and close your eyes, as many people traditionally do when praying, you can gain a measure of solitude. Prayer can be your link to God, who can respond to your prayers and change the circumstances causing stress. Prayer can also be a time of personal reflection that changes you: your attitude, perspective, standing with God, and future course of action.

Here are some tips on how to pray to relieve stress.

A Regular Event Pray regularly rather than just when under extreme stress. By making prayers a regular practice, you will enjoy ongoing benefits of meditation and personal reflection, and you will develop a close relationship with God. When you have a familiar relationship with God, you will have more faith that God is hearing your prayers and will respond when you are stressed.

Thanks   When you pray, express thanks to God for the good things in your life. Counting your blessings in prayer can put life's stressors into perspective so they are less overwhelming.

Wisdom   Ask God for wisdom. Sometimes life gets out of control, and you can't figure out how to change your life to reduce stress. At such times, ask God for the wisdom to reduce stress or manage the stress you cannot escape.

A Clear Conscience   Tell God about things you've done that you regret. Having a clear conscience goes a long way to relieve stress.

Worries   Hand over your cares. The Bible says, "Cast all your care upon Him [God], for He cares for you." When you pray, take all your cares and worries to God. List them one by one and ask God to take care of them. When these cares and worries begin to weigh on you again, remind yourself that they are in the capable hands of God.

Attitudes   Ask God to reveal anything in your attitudes and actions that needs to change. Then remain quiet as you listen to any prompting in your conscience about areas of your life that need to change.

A Child of God   Believe that God is listening and will answer your prayers. God tells us He is our Father in heaven. See yourself as God's child. There will be times you will ask your Father for something, and in His wisdom, the answer to your request will be no. Just because you don't always get what you request, don't stop praying. God may withhold things He knows would not be good for you in the long run.

Specific Requests Pray as specifically as possible. For example, instead of praying, "God, bless my friend," pray, "God, please help my friend find a job that will give her enough money to meet her monthly budget."

32 ✳ Listen to Something Soothing

The things you hear have a dramatic effect on your level of stress. If you are surrounded by a cacophony of unpleasant sounds, bickering voices, or other forms of noise pollution, you will probably experience stress as a result. Evidence from studies done in countries around the world shows a connecting link between high noise levels and stress-related illnesses.

Here are some ideas for controlling the things you hear.

Give Yourself a Respite from Noise

Arrange to have some quiet time each day. Turn off the TV, radio, tape player, and anything else that produces noise. Close your windows and doors to the noise of the outside world. If you can't have quiet at home, go somewhere you can. Try a library, chapel, or church.

Listen to Music That Gives You Pleasure

Choose music you enjoy. If competing noises interfere with your enjoyment of music, use earphones.

Listen to Tapes Specifically Designed to Relax You   Some tapes capture the soothing sounds of nature. There are recordings of waves crashing on the beach, birds chirping happily, a brook babbling through a wood, rain showering on the roof, thunderstorms booming, and waterfalls roaring, among other outdoor sounds.

Whenever you are feeling stressed, you can close your eyes, put your feet up, turn on one of these outdoor tapes, and let yourself take a momentary vacation from the pressures of the day.

Reduce the Noise Level at Work   If you are surrounded by unwanted noise at work, do what you can to reduce the noise level or remove yourself from the noise by changing the location of your work area.

Wear Earplugs   If you can't reduce the noise around you, reduce the noise you hear by wearing earplugs. Several styles of earplugs are quite comfortable. Check with your local pharmacist to find the style that makes you feel most comfortable while minimizing noise.

33 * Try Gardening

Gardening is a fulfilling way to relax and release tensions. Digging in the dirt can be a form of play. Breaking up fallow ground and pulling weeds can be nondestructive ways to let out your aggression. Planting beautiful flowers has an aesthetic effect. Tending your plants as they grow develops patience and allows you a break from the world, which demands instant results. Besides all of this, people who enjoy gardening will tell you that gardening is fun.

Gardening can be done alone if you feel the need to get away by yourself to relax. Or if you are looking for an activity for the entire family, gardening can be enjoyed by children and adults together.

Here are some ideas for gardening.

Plots or Pots? If you have a plot of ground, use a portion of it for your garden. Grow whatever you like that lends itself to your climate and soil conditions. Check with a local nursery when deciding what to plant. When you select vegetables, also keep in mind your favorites at mealtimes.

If you don't have a plot of ground, use pots that you can place on a patio or windowsill to create a garden of flowers, fruits, or vegetables.

Enjoy a houseplant or an herb garden that fits inside your kitchen window.

Make good use of your flower beds. Plant flowers to bloom in all seasons.

Leafy Pleasure If you don't have a garden but you do have trees, try raking leaves for relaxation. The combination of exercise, fresh air, and the beauty of being out in nature can reduce tensions. If you want to have some fun afterward, try playing with the leaves you've raked. If you need instruction, any child can show you how to make the best use of a pile of leaves.

Learning Time If you don't know how to garden, there are several ways to learn:

- Ask someone you know who has a garden. Gardeners are usually eager to talk about their hobby and share their expertise. A walk around your neighborhood may lead you to someone who takes pride in gardening.

- Read books or magazines from your local library that deal with gardening. There are resources for the novice as well as the seasoned gardener. Your librarian can direct you to the resources you need.

- Visit your local plant nursery and ask the proprietor to suggest the plants that would work for your circumstances.

- Visit or join a garden club in your community. You

can locate them by checking with your local plant nursery or checking club listings in a community newspaper.

- Subscribe to a gardening magazine.

34 ✳ Enjoy the Beauty of Nature

Something about the beauty of nature has a therapeutic effect. Being outdoors in a pleasant surrounding can put the stresses of life into perspective. The following suggestions can guide anyone to the beauty of nature. Some of these suggestions may require more time or travel than you can afford, but others can be enjoyed anywhere and in brief moments.

Water Sit on the beach and watch the waves crashing on the shore.

Sit on a riverbank and watch the water flow to the sea.

Mountains Go to the mountains. Hike or climb. Play in the snow or roll down a grassy hill.

Clouds Lie on your back and watch the clouds floating by. Try to imagine what the shapes represent.

Flowers Experience a flower. Don't just give it a passing glance. Really look to see the shape, the symmetry, and the various colors. Look at tiny flowers you find randomly in the grass, and allow yourself to appreciate the loveliness at your feet. Stop to smell the roses. Touch and feel the velvety softness of the petals. Take a walk (even just around the block) and focus your attention on each flower you see.

Insects   Watch insects. Look at ladybugs. Follow a caterpillar to see where it goes. Lift up a rock and consider the tiny world beneath it. Take a walk with the intention of noticing all the insects along the way.

Birds   Watch birds. Bird-watching can be interesting, educational, and fun, with or without binoculars. Look to see how many birds you can find. Watch them in flight. Listen to their songs.

Don't put off enjoying nature until you have a vacation. Even if you live and work in the city, you can find the beauty of nature where you are. Pay attention to the trees, the flowers, the sky. Reflecting on their beauty will take your mind off your pressures and help you relax.

35 ✳ Don't Make Commitments You Can't Keep

Stress is often created when you are confronted with your inability to live up to your commitments. These commitments may take the form of financial debt where you commit yourself to regular payments beyond your means. You may get involved in a business relationship where you are unable to live up to the terms of the agreement. You may agree to time schedules that don't mesh with your lifestyle or other time commitments. Perhaps you enter into a committed personal relationship where the expectations of the other person create demands that prove to be too much. All of these kinds of stress originate with an initial commitment on your part.

You can greatly reduce stress by understanding where you have overcommitted yourself in the past and changing your ways. Here are some specific ideas to help you release yourself from commitments that are too much for you to bear easily.

Know Yourself and Your Limitations If you understand your personal style in terms of finances, time management, and interpersonal relationships, you can more easily determine if a commitment is too much for you. Make commitments that accommodate your limitations. For example, if you seem to always run late, don't commit yourself to be the one who opens the doors for other employees at your job.

Get a Handle on People Pleasing

Many individuals enter into commitments because they want to please people. People pleasers have a hard time saying no to anyone or any commitment asked of them because they fear displeasing others. If you tend toward saying yes when you really should say no, find out why. It may be as simple as reevaluating your life, becoming aware of this pattern, and choosing to say no when you need to. If you can't stop overcommitting yourself because of a fear of rejection or some other related issue, you may want to speak with a counselor about the issue.

The reality of the situation is that your desire to please may prompt you to say yes, but your limitations may keep you from being able to live up to the commitment. When your inability to keep your commitment becomes evident, the person you were trying to please will not be pleased. And you may experience undue stress, which you could have avoided from the beginning.

Keep a Written Record of Your Commitments

Record all your commitments, then consult this record before you add more of them. You may enter into commitments without thinking through how each individual commitment fits with the others you have already made. Include the basic role commitments that form the foundation of your life, such as parent, spouse, child caring for an elderly parent, and so on. Next to each recorded commitment, note what it requires of you in terms of time, energy, or money. It will help you see when you cross the line and end up trying to do too much.

Get an Objective Opinion Ask an objective person who knows you and cares for your well-being to give you an opinion about taking on new commitments. Whenever you are about to add a new commitment, show this person your written record, listen to the person's comments, and incorporate them into your decision-making process. Sometimes your desire to do something may cloud your realism. Having someone who is not emotionally involved in the decision can help you be more realistic.

Learn to Say No If you don't know how to say no, you will end up in situations with an overload of stress. The reason is that those who never say no get a reputation for always being available. They get asked to help much more than others. Whenever volunteers are needed for special projects at work, whenever the school needs someone to bake cookies, whenever a friend needs a helping hand, those who never say no will be at the top of the list to call. Therefore, a cycle is created that will eventually lead to overload until you learn to say no.

Saying no is not really as hard as you might think. You don't have to go into any long explanation about why you can't do whatever is asked of you. Just say, "No, I'm sorry I'm not available." Try it a few times. It gets easier with practice.

36 * Stop Doing Too Much

If you are doing too much, you will continually battle stress. Doing too much creates time pressures, keeps you from getting the rest and recreation you need, and diminishes the quality of family and other personal relationships. With the ongoing pressure of never feeling caught up, the fatigue, and the lack of quality time for building relationships with those you love, you are likely to become irritable. That further undermines the quality of your life and work. One way to defuse this stressful cycle is to cut back on what you are doing.

Here are some ideas to help you stop doing too much.

Recognize That You Are Doing Too Much

How much is too much? Well, that depends on each individual. However, consider some indicators. You are consistently forced to rush. You don't have time to listen to your child when he is trying to tell you something. You are always behind on your projects and commitments. Your loved ones complain that you don't have time for them. Whenever you are supposed to be playing or relaxing, you are hounded by thoughts of what you should be doing that is not getting done. You are having sleep difficulties. You experience frequent or ongoing fatigue.

You are irritable. You never completely catch up. If these indicators are present in your life, you may be doing more than you can handle.

Set Clear Priorities   Before you can start cutting back on what you are doing, you need to clarify the relative importance of your tasks. Make a list of all the things you spend your time and energy doing. Then arrange them in order from most to least important.

Cut Back on Low-Priority Items   Choose to stop doing those things that are of relatively little importance. Communicate with whoever else is affected by your decision to cut back, or change your level of involvement in a particular activity.

Change Your Life-Style   Consider possible lifestyle changes that would relieve you of the pressure to do too much. If you find that you are doing too much because you must to meet the needs of your family, as in the case of a single parent, consider how you might reach out for more support so that you are relieved of some of the pressure. If you must work grueling hours to keep up with the standard of living you enjoy, consider whether you could live more simply so that the financial demands are not as great. If you are doing too much during this season of life because you are striving to reach a goal within a set time limit, consider allowing yourself additional time. For example, if you are working and going to school full-time to graduate in four years, consider allowing yourself to graduate in six years by carrying a lighter class load.

37 ✴ Have a Good Cry

Have you ever felt much better after a good cry? Well, there may be a sound scientific explanation for that. Crying when emotionally distraught or under great stress can actually help restore the chemical balance in your body. The book *Managing Stress* reports,

> Chemical analysis of tears shed by people watching emotionally upsetting movies compared to those of people exposed to onion vapors shows that the emotional tears contain significantly greater levels of protein. Tears, in theory, may help remove chemicals that build up during an emotionally stressful situation, thereby restoring the body's chemical balance.

Other studies have shown that control groups of persons who are not ashamed to cry are less prone to stress-related illnesses than persons who view crying as a sign of weakness. This evidence demonstrates what you may know from experience: crying can make you feel better in a stressful situation.

Think about tears. They flow from within us: cleansing, refreshing, relaxing, and carrying away our sadness. It's almost as though our tears wash away some of our overwhelming feelings. People talk of drowning in their emotions. The tears flowing out can keep you from drowning by releasing some of the emotional pressure.

Sometimes people are confronted with overwhelming emotional stress that makes it hard to express feelings in words. At times when words can't capture the emotions, crying is a way to release these emotions. They may be tears of grief, loss, fear, pain, sadness, happiness, or anger. At times when words fail us, our tears may become eloquent.

Here are some tips on having a good cry.

Make Yourself Cry Instead of avoiding the emotional triggers that surface difficult emotions, expose yourself to the things that help your emotions come to the surface. These triggers might be photographs, aromas, places with special symbolic meaning for your life, letters, notes, music re-creating a mood, or just a sad movie or song.

Allow Yourself a Safe Place to Cry Find a friend who offers a shoulder to cry on. Go to your room and cry into a pillow. Take a walk along the beach. If you are around people who shame you for crying, the positive release you get from crying will be counteracted by the additional stress created by their negative reactions.

Don't Fight Your Tears When you feel like crying, don't try to stuff your feelings down or artificially make yourself forget your true feelings. Instead, let yourself get the feelings out with your tears. Then you can do something to make yourself feel better.

38 ✳ Escape with a Good Book

Reading has always been a great escape. Publishing was one of the few industries that fared well during the Great Depression, and it continues to grow during times of recession. The reason is that as stress grows in times of economic difficulty, people reduce their stress by reading.

Here are some ideas for escaping with a good book.

Choose the Kind of Book You Most Enjoy

To be able to escape the pressures surrounding you, choose a book that catches your interest. You can select from action-adventures, mysteries, romances, historical fiction, humor, science fiction, psychological thrillers, westerns, and other kinds of stories.

Read Condensed Books

If you say you have no time to read because of your pressing schedule, read condensed books rather than full-length editions.

Listen to a Book

If you are not one to enjoy reading or feel you don't have extra time to read, try listening to a book read on audiotape. It can help you relax as you listen to a story before going to bed or while driving home from work.

Keep a Book Beside Your Bed   If you have trouble turning your thoughts away from stressful pressures, try reading before going to sleep. Sometimes the switch to other thoughts will allow you to relax enough to get to sleep. If you awake during the night and are unable to go back to sleep, a book on the bedside table may keep your mind off concerns that might cause you to worry the night away.

Read Short Stories   If you don't enjoy reading full-length novels, try shorter readings. Keep a book of poetry, short stories, or inspirational quotes available to read whenever you are feeling stressed. Sometimes this reading break can provide a welcome respite in the midst of stressful circumstances without taking much time.

39 ✳ Get Some Help

When you are experiencing stress overload, you can reduce stress by getting some help. Stress caused by too much to do, too many commitments, or excessive demands on your time and energy can be reduced by having someone take over some of your duties. Emotional stress can be relieved by sharing your sorrows with others who understand or by getting the assistance of a professional counselor. Stress created by financial difficulties can be relieved by receiving advice from a financial counselor who shows you how to redesign your financial situation. Financial stress can also be reduced by a well-timed bonus or a loan that gives you a buffer in your situation.

Here are some tips for getting help when you are stressed.

Ask for Help   If you realize you are overloaded, ask someone who cares for you to lend a hand. You might say something like, "I could really use your help. I've gotten myself in over my head, and I'm feeling the stress. Could you please help me find some slack by doing a few errands?"

Be Specific   People are much more likely to help out if you specify what they can do. They may not know where to start or what you have on your unfinished agenda that is causing you stress. Take a moment to identify what you are worrying about having to do or what you feel unable to accomplish. Then you can ask people to take over one of the things on your list.

Express Appreciation   Be sure to express appreciation for the act and the effect. Whenever someone helps you out by doing something that reduces the stress level, thank the person for the action and for what the action has done for you. You might say something like, "Thank you for taking those packages to the post office. Knowing that was taken care of allowed me to finish this project without being distracted by the worry that I would miss the mail deadline."

Seek Skilled Help   Seek help from those who are skilled at dealing with what is causing your stress. Identify what you suspect to be the source of your stress, then find appropriate help for the root of stress in your life. If you are in constant conflict with your spouse, seek the help of a qualified marriage counselor. If you are struggling with other family-related problems, contact an organization such as Focus on the Family for qualified referrals. If unmanageable debt is raising your stress level, consult a financial counselor. If you are physically ill, get treatment from your physician. When you face a problem with the help of someone trained to deal with that problem, you will probably get the results you need.

40 ✷ Link into Your Community

Some situations that would be easily manageable as an active member of a community can become highly stressful when you are not linked into your community. That is one reason relocating can be stressful. You have to reconnect with a new community. Loneliness and isolation can also create or contribute to feelings of stress. When you must face your problems on your own, when you feel that no one understands or cares about the pressures of your life, when you feel cut off from others or out of touch with those around you, life will be more stressful than it would if you were linked into a caring community.

Here are some ways linking into your community can help you reduce stress.

Interdependence and a Sense of Belonging
You are in a position to help others and have them help you. Community involvement allows you to find a sense of belonging. When you get involved with others who share common interests, you will feel that you belong in the groups with whom you associate. Some possibilities to consider include a place of worship, community service organizations, volunteer service organizations, support groups, and family-related groups, such as parenting classes, PTA, or Scouting.

Resources Within your community you can identify resources to meet your needs. As you link into your community, you will find health care, educational resources, spiritual resources, entertainment, and so on. Having these resources identified gives you a greater sense of security and the assurance of knowing where to turn in times of need.

Friendship Within your community you can develop positive relationships with friends and neighbors.

Personal Significance You can make a difference through community involvement. Sometimes stress is accentuated by feelings of helplessness. For example, you may feel stress over the growing rate of crime in your neighborhood. By becoming involved with others in your community in working toward a common goal, you gain a sense of control over your life. Heading up or joining a neighborhood watch chapter would reduce stress by facing off with the source of stress.

The Link Here are some ideas on how to link into your community:

- Attend meetings related to things of interest to you. You might choose a meeting of parents, church members, members of your political party, or people who share your hobby.

- Consult your local Chamber of Commerce or newcomers group.

- Look for resources through the phone directory.

- Invite your neighbors over for a cup of tea.
- Get to know the parents of your children's friends.
- Volunteer your services to an organization of interest.

41 * Develop and Draw from Friendships

A good friend can provide stress relief. When you know someone is on your side, you can draw on the love for you when you feel the need. Just being able to call someone you know will not judge you harshly when you are under pressure helps immensely.

Here are some ideas on how to develop and draw from friendships when you are under stress.

Make Time for Your Friends Schedule in times for friendship if you don't seem to make time automatically. If you don't have time to spend with your friends, the friendships may wane.

Be Available for Your Friends Make yourself available for your friends when they are under stress and need help. Try to do what you can to encourage them, give an objective view of their situation, offer advice when asked, and provide practical help when you can. In friendship, as in all of life, you will get back what you give out. If you are there for your friends when they are under stress, they will be there for you.

Turn to Fun Friends   Take a break with friends who are fun to be around. When you are stressed, call a friend with whom you feel comfortable. If possible, see if the two of you can do something enjoyable—take a hike, ride your bikes, or whatever.

Talk Out Your Problems with Your Friend

Sometimes a friend can see a way to make changes that would reduce the stress level in your life. Knowledge of you and your life-style may give the person the right perspective from which to offer beneficial suggestions.

Work Out Difficulties in the Relationship Quickly   Being at odds with a friend can create stress.

Make a habit of talking openly with your friends about difficulties in the relationship and resolving them right away.

Choose Positive Friends   Choose friends who build you up instead of tearing you down. If you are surrounded by friends who are continually criticizing you or spouting pessimism, don't continue to spend your free time with them as long as they have such negative attitudes. Instead, choose friends whose company lifts you up and encourages you in positive ways.

42 ＊ Reduce Perfectionist Demands on Yourself

No human being is perfect, and that includes you. Therefore, if you demand perfection of yourself, you are creating a life situation where you will live with constant stress. This stress can come from constant feelings of failure because your standards are unattainable. Stress can also come from driving yourself too hard when trying to achieve or maintain perfection.

Your perfectionist demands may come from someone else. You may have grown up in a family where your acceptance within the family was based on your performance rather than your inherent value as a person. You may be married to someone who has in mind an ideal of the perfect spouse, and your partner is trying to make you conform to this image. You may be a member of a team or peer group requiring conformity that is out of reach for you as you are.

In these situations and many others, perfectionist demands cause you to fear rejection. They may also cause you to strive for conformity to the demands of others, which takes its toll in other areas of your life. For example, trying to compete on the job and become the perfect corporate employee may compromise your ability to fulfill your roles at home. If you are also striving to be the perfect parent, you may find yourself in a no-win situation;

your perfectionism sets you at odds against yourself in your various roles.

Here are some ideas for dealing with perfectionism.

Admit to Yourself That You Are Not Perfect

Recognize your human limitations. If you cannot easily see your human limitations, ask someone close to you to point them out. These limitations apply to time, attention, energy, intellectual and physical abilities, finances, and so on.

Change Your Aim

Instead of aiming to be perfect in your particular roles (and then bemoaning how far you fall short of perfection), identify where you are now and aim for measurable improvement. You will get positive momentum to move forward without the weight of stress produced when you see yourself always falling short.

Don't Promise Perfection

Tell others you will not always live up to their expectations. Others may demand perfection of you in terms of the image they want to mold you into. Decide what you are aiming for in your life. Then tell others seeking to shape your life that you will not always mold yourself to their designs. If that is a dynamic at work within your family, one pronouncement will probably not change a lifetime of relational patterns. You must follow up by not giving in to the demands of others when their demands are not in keeping with your personal goals. You may need the guidance of a professional family therapist to learn these skills.

Reward Yourself Reward yourself for progress rather than punish yourself for imperfection. For example, if you get five *A*'s and two *B*'s, reward yourself for the *A*'s and take note of improvements.

43 ✳ Motivate Yourself with Attainable Goals

Having attainable goals can reduce stress in numerous ways. Here are some of them.

Move Away from Perfectionism Attainable goals are a healthy alternative to perfectionist demands. By setting goals and giving yourself a reasonable amount of time to reach them, you can reduce the pressure of feeling that you should already have attained them. While you are working toward a goal, you can keep your perfectionism at bay by reminding yourself that you are actively pursuing being and doing your best in a particular area.

Maintain Balance When you have clearly defined goals, you give yourself a structure for expending your energy. All attainable goals include a plan and a time line for fulfilling the plan. By adhering to the time line, you can keep life manageable by balancing hard work and adequate rest. Without a plan for the accomplishment of a goal, you may end up nearing a deadline and having to work night and day to complete the goal in time.

Handle Disappointments Having attainable goals helps you deal with disappointments. When you are focused on having attainable goals for every area of life, your personal fulfillment isn't perceived as coming from only one source. Therefore, if you experience a setback in any area of life, it is not as though your entire life is falling apart. By having your goals clearly defined, you can accept a disappointment and devise a plan to get your life back on track.

Set Attainable Goals Set goals for all areas of life: personal, career, family, social, financial, and spiritual.

In each area consider your longings and dreams for the future:

- Make a list of things you wish for in your life.

- Prioritize the wishes that are most important to you. Pinpoint three top priorities.

- Identify the obstacles that stand between you and your three top-priority desires.

- Determine where you can find help to overcome these obstacles.

- Devise a plan to overcome these obstacles, which starts from where you are now and takes into account the resources you have available to help you fulfill your plan.

- Set a date for reaching your goal, then plot your time backward to the present. Make sure you give yourself manageable steps that will fit with the current demands of your life-style. Then incorporate time each day to work toward your goal.

Write your goals in specific terms.

Review your goals regularly. Look at your short-term goals every night before bed. Look at your intermediate goals at least once per week, perhaps when you check your calendar for the coming week. Look at your long-range goals at least once each year. A good time to review all goals is between Christmas and New Year's Day.

44 ✳ Play

Play and stress don't easily coexist. When you are involved in playful relaxation, your mind is diverted from troubles and pressures. However, people who tend to live under stress often find it difficult to incorporate play into their life-styles. Perhaps the time demands causing a great deal of stress don't leave time for play, as in the case of a single parent who works and has custody of small children. Or troubling life changes that cause stress, such as a death or divorce in the family, may leave you emotionally distraught. At times of high emotional stress you probably won't feel like playing, or you may think that play is inappropriate during a time of grief.

Whatever the causes of your stress, you can help yourself reduce its negative effects if you allow yourself to play. Here are some suggestions.

Schedule Time with Fun-Loving People
You know which friends know how to play. If you are feeling especially stressed, ask them to become your play therapists. Schedule time to be with them, and let them plan the events. Be sure your playtime doesn't rely on alcohol or other recreational drugs. They may make you feel better momentarily, but they can act as depressants or end up putting more stress on your system.

Take Play Breaks Play in little ways that give you momentary breaks from the stress. Try to incorporate games into your life. You can even play solitaire or computer games by yourself. Work a crossword puzzle. Play board games with your children. Play relational games that get you involved with other people (such as Pictionary, Trivial Pursuit, or Balderdash).

Schedule Play Schedule playtime into each day and week. Make playing a regular part of your life-style. Set aside time for fun activities with your family. Have a weekly time for family outings. Go roller-skating, bowling, or kite flying with children. Have a picnic or go for a hike in the woods.

Play Before You Feel Like Playing Don't wait to feel like playing before you begin. Commit yourself to play. Once you begin to play, your stress level will decrease, and you will feel more like playing.

Look at Play as Time Well Spent If you worry about losing time from work by playing, don't! You will probably be better able to work and think clearly after being refreshed by play.

45 ✻ Reduce Worry

Worry is experiencing stress over something that hasn't happened yet. When you worry, your body reacts to your anticipation of danger or catastrophe as though it already occurred. Consider the degree of stress children go through when they anticipate getting a shot from the doctor. Although nothing has hurt them physically, they may become hysterical and experience tremendous stress from what they are afraid will happen. You do the same thing when you worry. You recall those things that have hurt you in the past, you recall the danger signals that foretold the pain, and you draw conclusions that you may be hurt again. Then you react to the fear of what may happen.

This ability to learn from past experiences can help you avoid pain if you use it in a positive way: by taking precautions that may protect you, by avoiding truly dangerous situations, or by altering your course of action to take care of yourself. However, if you allow yourself to give in to worry, you create extra stress for yourself without doing much good.

Here are some ways to reduce your tendency to worry.

Clarify What Is Reality   If you are waiting up for a teenager who is late coming home from a date, the reality is that the teen is late. Your mind may run through a host of potentially terrible reasons for what is making the teen late. These possible catastrophes are not reality. Remind yourself of the facts.

Keep All Possibilities in Mind   When you begin to worry about all the possible scenarios of what may happen in potentially dangerous situations, also remind yourself of the other possibilities. If your spouse is acting evasive and you fear something terrible, that evasive behavior could be hiding a special surprise for you. When you begin to worry, you may reduce stress by making two lists of possible outcomes for whatever you are worried about. On one list, write the possible negative outcomes or explanations. On the other, write the possible positive outcomes or explanations.

Talk It Out   Talk about your worries with someone who has a positive attitude. Sometimes another person can help you ward off worries from which you just can't seem to shake free.

46 ✳ Be Creative

Sometimes being creative seems to take your mind off those things that stress you out. There is good reason for this. Research shows that the brain is divided into two hemispheres. In very basic terms, the right side of your brain deals with analytical, problem-solving tasks, and the left side deals with more creative functions. When you switch to using the creative side of your brain, you literally take a break from analyzing your problems or focusing on the pressures that may be causing you stress.

Learn from Leaders Throughout history, great leaders escaped the pressures of having the world's problems on their shoulders by pursuing some creative outlet of their talents. A noteworthy example is Sir Winston Churchill. In *The Last Lion,* William Manchester refers to the stress-reducing powers of creative expression as Churchill viewed them:

Eddie Marsh, who watched his [Churchill's] first efforts [at painting], thought that "the new enthusiasm . . . was a distraction and a sedative that brought a measure of ease to his frustrated spirit." In fact, it would be a solace to him for the next fifty years. He had, he believed, discovered the solution to anxiety and tension. Exercise, travel, retreat, solitude, forced gaiety —he had tried these and none had worked. "Change," [Churchill] now wrote, "is the master key. A man can wear out a particular part of his mind by continually using it and tiring it. . . . The tired parts of the mind can be rested and strengthened, not merely by rest, but by using other parts. . . . It is only when new cells are called into activity, when new stars become lords of the ascendant, that relief, repose, refreshment are afforded."

If you have yet to find a form of creative expression you enjoy, keep looking. You may want to take a class to get you started.

Choose One—or More   Here are some forms of creative expression you may want to try:

- Painting, sketching, or drawing
- Sewing, crocheting, or knitting
- Writing poetry or other creative works
- Singing, songwriting, or playing a musical instrument
- Dancing or miming
- Building things: models, sand castles, structures
- Making sculptures and pottery
- Cooking and baking
- Doing crafts

47 ✴ Rid Yourself of Spiritual Stressors

When you are contending with an inner spiritual battle, you will experience stress regardless of the circumstances in your outer life. Someone asked a prolific author how he was able to produce so much high-quality material. His answer included the expected tips on time management and organization. However, he also credited the fact that he maintained a low-stress inner life. He did that by making sure no internal spiritual issues were distracting him, sapping his energy or attention away from his work.

You, too, can reduce the level of stress you experience and perhaps increase your productivity by ridding yourself of the following spiritual stressors:

- Unforgiveness toward yourself and others

- Bitterness

- Grudges

- A guilty conscience

Here are some tips for ridding yourself of these spiritual stressors.

Learn to Forgive Others Forgiveness does not mean acting as though what was done against you was acceptable. Forgiveness involves first acknowledging the wrong committed (or the right action omitted), then choosing to give up your demands that the other person make it up to you for what happened. Instead, you choose to turn the matter over to higher authorities; it could be God or civil authorities if laws have been broken.

Receive Forgiveness There are times when you have failed or fallen short of what is the right thing to do. When your failures or shortcomings have negative effects for you or those you love, you may find it difficult to believe that God or others can still accept you.

You may be better able to believe that God accepts you in spite of your mistakes if you clearly understand the process. Check with your minister or a member of the clergy to help you learn how to receive the forgiveness God offers.

If you have trouble receiving forgiveness from others, it may help to make amends for the negative effects of your choices and behavior. Admit the wrongs you have committed and the rights you have omitted to the people involved (as long as this admission won't further harm anyone). Then do whatever you can to make up for any pain or inconvenience you may have caused.

Forgive Yourself After you have received forgiveness from God and others, let yourself off the hook. It does no good to go on beating yourself up for past mistakes and failures. Instead, list the things you hold against yourself. After each one, note any changes you can make that will keep you from repeating the offense. Do what you can to make your future better than the past and leave the past behind.

Let Go of Grudges and Bitterness Make a list of everyone you hold a grudge against and the action that offended you. Make a conscious decision to mend each relationship. If you have never told the individuals that you are offended, go to them and discuss whatever has disturbed you. Go with the desire to repair the relationship, not with the goal of showing them how discourteous they have been. State what happened (to your understanding) and why that upset you. Listen to whatever they have to say by way of explanation. Then be willing to forgive them for past offenses. It may take time for the relationship to resume as it was before the offense. In the meantime, show them kindness as an act of your will until the kind feelings return.

Clear Your Conscience Your conscience can help you by pointing out whenever you cross the line between right and wrong. Pay attention to your conscience. If you hear that small inner voice warning you away from something, listen and obey.

If you are carrying around a weight of guilt because you are doing things that violate your conscience, you could benefit from an old-fashioned dose of repentance. To repent simply means to recognize where you are wrong, then change your mind about what you are doing and choose to go a different direction, specifically in the direction of what you know to be right.

You should repent whenever you violate your conscience. By keeping the list of offenses short, you will ease your mind and reduce the level of stress you experience whenever you are in the midst of an internal moral battle.

48 ✳ See Your Doctor

Although the causes of stress are varied, all stress produces a physical effect. Stress is known to cause a suppression of the immune response. When you are under a high level of stress, your immune system is not able to function as it should to protect you. Therefore, you are more vulnerable to infectious diseases. Stress may also be a significant factor in heart disease, headaches, backaches, stomach and digestive disorders, skin rashes, hypertension, and even sexual dysfunction. If you are under an unmanageable level of stress, seek medical care for your physical well-being. Make an appointment for a checkup with your doctor.

A Prescription for Better Health   There are several ways your doctor can help you reduce stress and/or the negative effects of stress, including the following:

- A medical doctor can prescribe medication, which helps your body better handle the physical effects of stress.

- Your doctor can teach you relaxation techniques.

- Your doctor can put your mind at ease if you are worried that high levels of stress may be endangering your health. Having a complete physical examination during seasons of extreme stress can either identify stress-related illness or relieve your mind of worry over the possibility of stress-related illness. If there are specific health problems, your doctor can address them medically.

- Your doctor may be able to refer you to other sources of help for your stressful situation.

49 ✱ Get Organized

Chaos and stress go together. When your life, house, and office are in order, your days will flow more smoothly. Life will become more predictable. When your life, house, and office are out of order, you are inviting a crisis of one sort or another. Therefore, you can reduce the likelihood of facing stress on a daily basis by getting organized.

Here are some ideas for organizing your life to reduce stress.

Organize Your Time Plan time commitments to minimize surprises. If you anticipate scheduling problems in advance, you can plan ahead to keep from having pressing time constraints (which are always stressful). Keep one calendar that integrates all your commitments. If you keep more than one calendar (say, one for home and another for work), you run the risk of forgetting to record an appointment in both places. Then you'll have conflicts you'll have to deal with later.

Organize Your Desk Organize your work space so that you have everything you need to do your job at your fingertips. Preplanning and maintaining a work space that meets your needs keep you from having to scramble to find things when you are trying to get your work done.

Rid Home, Car, and Office of Clutter If you have a tendency to collect clutter, you may need to hire a professional to streamline your belongings. Or you may be able to declutter your life by following the instructions in various self-help organizational books on the market.

Organize Your Home Organize your home so that it is easy to perform your daily routines. Consider the function of each area of your home, and organize the space to help you enjoy life. See your closet as a space where you get dressed easily each day. This new view will encourage you to move everything out of your closet that doesn't help you get dressed. For example, if wrapping paper is on the upper shelf of your closet (and often falls down when you are trying to find your favorite suit), move it to another place designed for gift wrapping. A better place might be in an office area or near the dining room table if that is the place used to wrap gifts.

50 ✳ Stick to a Routine

Stress is associated with life changes and the potential insecurity these changes represent. Whenever there is a high level of stress in your life, you can counteract the negative effects by maintaining routines. One clear illustration of the calming effects of routines can be seen in children. Whenever young children experience a major life change, there will usually be a stress reaction. If a young child is separated from one or both parents, the child may regress to behavior from an earlier stage of development. The child may adopt comforting habits from the past, such as thumb sucking or taking a bottle. In such situations, one of the best ways to reduce the level of stress is to maintain as much routine as possible. The routines associated with waking, dressing, bathing, playtime, naptime, and bedtime give a sense of normalcy in an abnormal situation. That is why a familiar blanket or toy takes on added importance to a child when life seems stressful.

Adults' stress reactions and attempts to find comfort when faced with life changes are similar. Adults, as well as children, find comfort in what is familiar and routine. Whenever there is an absence of predictable routines, life will be more stressful. Consider how having a job that requires working unpredictable hours tends to be more stressful than a job that requires working the same number of predictable hours. You can minimize stress by creating dependable routines.

Here are some ways you can maximize the calming effects of having a routine for your life.

In the Evening   Have a set time to go to bed each night.

Before you retire for bed, observe a calming bedtime routine. Perhaps have a warm drink (without caffeine), read, pray, or listen to relaxing music.

In the Morning   Wake at a set time each morning.

Practice a morning routine designed to reduce stress. Wake up with plenty of time to do what you need to do before your daily obligations begin. Give yourself time for stretching or exercising, reflecting quietly, reading the newspaper, or watching the morning news before your workday begins.

Groom yourself in the same way and in the same place each day. You may want to wake up or groom yourself to the same music each day.

Throughout the Week   Keep a basic daily and weekly schedule that is predictable, flexible, and tailored to your needs. For example, use the morning for uninterrupted work, return calls in the early afternoon, and answer mail at day's end. This general guideline for your routine will help you keep your equilibrium, even at times when your specific plans are upset by unexpected events.

Plan to make the most of high-energy times and

demand the least of yourself when your energy level is low.

Spend time in familiar places. If you have a favorite spot that makes you feel secure, go there on a regular basis.

51 ✳ Practice the Serenity Prayer

The Serenity Prayer in the popular version used today says,

> God,
> Grant me the serenity
> to accept the things I cannot change,
> the courage to change the things I can,
> and the wisdom to know the difference. Amen.

These simple lines have helped untold millions of people learn to manage stress in their lives. You, too, can find solace in praying the Serenity Prayer and practicing the principles it teaches.

Here is how practicing the Serenity Prayer can help you reduce stress.

Acknowledgment It helps you acknowledge there are some things in life beyond your control. When you recognize that something is beyond your control, you are free to stop trying to change it. Fighting futile battles is exhausting and stressful.

Encouragement It encourages constructive action to direct your life in positive ways. When you see yourself as a helpless victim, you will be more prone to stress. Helpless victims live in danger and therefore experience continual stress out of fear of what may happen to them next. When you identify things you can do to change your life for the better and summon the courage to change, you release yourself from the role of a victim.

Wisdom It puts you in touch with God and opens you up to receive God-granted wisdom. In many stressful situations you may not know what course of action would help you reduce the stress you are experiencing. When you ask God for wisdom, you may be surprised to find that it comes to you. You may discover possible ways of life leading you out of stress overload that you never saw previously.

Prayerfulness Even if you are not someone who prays regularly, you can learn to pray the Serenity Prayer. Here are several ways you can do so:

- Memorize the prayer and recite it aloud during a quiet time. Then spend a few moments reflecting on what you need to accept that you cannot change contrasted with those things that can be changed, even though they require courage.

- Pray the prayer silently whenever you are in a stressful situation.

- Pray the prayer with someone close to you as a routine part of your day, either in the morning or at day's end.

52 ✻ Identify and Eliminate Specific Stressors

When you are feeling stressed and want to reduce the negative effects of stress in a given situation, you must first identify the specific stressors in your life. They will fall into two categories: things you can change and things you have no power to change. Once you have identified a list of specific stress points that are within your power to change, you can take action to eliminate each one or reduce the negative effects produced.

Here are some tips on how you can go about identifying and eliminating specific stressors.

Make a List List everything in your life that you perceive as causing stress. If you are not sure, start by referring to the list of stressors given in the Introduction. Note anything in the past year that had a stressful effect. Then think through your past week and identify the relationships, settings, and times you felt the effects of stress. List them on a sheet of paper.

Evaluate the List Draw a line through the items that are beyond your power to change at this time. For example, some of the items you would cross off as being stressful but beyond your power to change would be the birth of a baby, the death of a loved one, graduation, adjustment to a new job, and so on.

Review the Remaining Items
These are ones you have the power to change in some way. Look for ways you could make changes that would eliminate the stress or make it more manageable. For example, if you listed "arguments with spouse over finances," think of several things you could do to make changes that might reduce stress in this area. Options might include increasing income, revising the budget, getting financial counseling, changing one spouse's or both spouses' expectations, and so on. For each stress point, create a list of options that you could take to reduce stress in that particular situation.

Set Specific Goals
Identify goals that can eliminate or reduce stress for each specific item on your list. You may not be able to eliminate or learn to manage the source of stress in your life immediately. However, by knowing clearly the stress points that you can change, you are able to move in the direction of a life where stress is reduced, and the stress that you cannot reduce is manageable.